D0680505

KEEPING GOLDFISH

KEEPING GOLDFISH

Dick Mills

BLANDFORD PRESS
POOLE · DORSET

First published in the UK 1985 by Blandford Press,
Link House, West Street, Poole, Dorset BH15 1LL.

Copyright © 1985 Blandford Press Ltd.

Distributed in the United States by
Sterling Publishing Co., Inc.,
2 Park Avenue, New York, N.Y. 10016.

British Library Cataloguing in Publication Data

Mills, Dick
   Keeping goldfish.
   1. Goldfish
   I. Title
   639.3′752   SF458.G6

ISBN 0 7137 1508 1 *(Hardback edition)*
ISBN 0 7137 1693 2 *(Paperback edition)*

All rights reserved. No part of this book may
be reproduced or transmitted in any form or by
any means, electronic or mechanical, including
photocopying, recording or any information storage
and retrieval system, without permission in
writing from the Publisher.

Typeset by Megaron Typesetting, Bournemouth, Dorset.

Printed in Great Britain by R.J. Acford, Chichester

CONTENTS

ACKNOWLEDGEMENTS

The author provided photographs for Figures 29, 34 and 38. Other sources, which the author and publisher gratefully acknowledge are as follows:

D. Allison: Figure 23;
Aquila: Figures 30 (M. Gilroy), 35, 36 (M. Gilroy), 40;
Bob Esson: Figures 28, 33, 36;
Laurence E. Perkins: Figures 1, 2, 24, 26, 27, 31, 32, 39.

The line drawings were prepared by Anita Lawrence.

INTRODUCTION

The Goldfish must be the most commonly-kept fish in the world. Apart from the wild-caught 'tiddlers' of our youth, probably everyone's aquarium-keeping experiences has included keeping a Goldfish at one time or another – even if they later progressed to the more 'modern' tropical species.

The Goldfish has much to offer, at whatever level of seriousness you wish to conduct your fishkeeping activities. It is a hardy creature and, like any species of fish, will not make too many demands upon your time or labours. It also has the virtue of not being too expensive to buy or keep.

Figure 1. By combining suitably compatible plants, chemically inert rocks and gravel with colourful fishes an artistic living picture can be created.

Of course, once you begin to take a more serious interest in the hobby you will naturally look for improved quality in any new stock of fishes and, eventually, you may take up Goldfish breeding and specialise in the more advanced Fancy Varieties.

Despite its having been around for many years (many centuries would be a more accurate assessment), the Goldfish is still looked on by most people as a starting point, rather than as a complete interest in itself. If only this narrow-mindedness could be eradicated, then more fishkeepers would come nearer to realising the fish's potential as a full-time proposition.

Within the limited space of this book, it is hoped to bring you a fuller coverage of the attractions and challenges of Goldfishkeeping than is usually found in aquarium manuals, so that you will not just pay lip-service to the Goldfish which, after all, has managed to survive as a hobbyist's fish for very many years.

HISTORY

The keeping of Goldfish has its origins in the Orient and was described in Chinese manuscripts of the Sung era in AD 1000. The fish also figures very strongly in earlier poetry, folklore and mythology, in which its characteristics of strength, courage and virility were admired and, at that time, adopted as ideals for male children.

It required some passage of time for the Goldfish to reach the rest of the world, and probably 500 years elapsed before the first spread outwards occurred; this was even further eastwards – to Japan. Here, its cultivation was further intensified and became a serious occupation. It was during these early stages of its breeding in captivity that the development of the familiar varieties we know today began.

Once trade routes were established between Europe and the Far East, it was only natural that species of these 'coloured fishes' should find their way westwards, and several records note the arrival of the Goldfish (and other exotic fishes) in Europe between the years 1611 and 1728. Goldfishes were soon being bred in Holland, after being introduced from Italy and England; in Russia, they were even used as decorations at a banquet for Catherine the Great in 1791. About a hundred years later, the North American continent was colonised and the Goldfish subsequently became recognised worldwide.

Introduction

TAXONOMY

It is generally agreed that the Goldfish evolved (ornamentally- rather than scientifically-speaking) from the more brightly-coloured individuals of the genus *Carassius*, a member of the Cyprinidae group – the Carps and Carp-like fishes. The genus contains, according to contemporary, taxonomic classification, two species: *Carassius carassius* (the Crucian Carp), and *C. auratus*, of which there are two subspecies – *C. auratus gibelio* (the Prussian Carp) and *C. auratus auratus* (the Goldfish).

Originally, the Goldfish was described by Linnaeus as *Cyprinus auratus*. Later, it was thought to be nothing more than a colour variant of *C. carassius,* and although a cursory visual examination would appear to support this, it is now accepted that the two fishes are, in fact, quite separate species.

Figure 2. If the dull bronze colour of this fish were to be changed to metallic red-orange, you would almost believe it was a Common Goldfish. However, it is a separate species, *Carassius carassius*, in its own right.

9

1

THE GOLDFISH AS AN AQUARIUM FISH

One of the virtues of the Goldfish is that it is a very versatile creature as far as fishkeeping is concerned. Although it can grow quite large, it appears to be quite happy in whatever situation it finds itself, acclimatising itself easily to either pond or aquarium. Of course, in this respect, it is assumed that the fish starts off life in captivity at the proper size relative to its surroundings and is not forced to live in cramped conditions, as would be the case should a large pond fish be brought indoors into a much smaller aquarium.

The advantages and disadvantages of keeping the Goldfish indoors, compared with allowing it a more natural life in an outdoor pond, need not be debated at too great a length. One of the main advantages is that you can see the fish at any time you wish, no matter what the weather or time of year. You can also study its behaviour and recognise signs of trouble that much earlier.

Against this, the fishes generally do not grow quite as large (their growth being limited by the dimensions of their aquarium), they may not attain such vibrant colours, nor receive as much natural live food or natural sunshine as do their counterparts in a pond. However, pond fishes usually need protection from predators and may well have to be brought indoors during the winter months anyway, when the more delicate varieties would be unable to survive the frosts or icy conditions.

Water conditions in the indoor aquarium should be more stable and controllable than those of the pond, which are at the mercy of vagaries in the weather and any pollution from manmade or natural sources. Similarly, all the other aspects of aquarium management (lighting, filtration, plants, feeding and breeding) are, or should be, under the much closer control of the fishkeeper.

Most people new to fishkeeping presume the Common Goldfish to be the only type of Goldfish that exists and it comes as quite a surprise to them to learn of the many other varieties that can be kept in the aquarium. There is a wide range of varieties from which to choose, and you would be very wise to settle on one particular variety rather than try to keep a mixture of fishes.

Figure 3. Common Goldfish: This orange-red metallic-scaled fish should be a sturdy, almost stocky, fish with the dorsal curve an exact 'mirror image' of the ventral surface.

Goldfish may be divided into two distinct groups – *Singletails* and *Twintails*. Fishes termed Singletails, as their name suggests, may be recognised by their tails and anal fins; these are the ordinary-looking, and ordinarily-formed, fins as found on any other fishes, whereas the Twintailed varieties have tails and anal fins that are double-sided or divided when seen from the rear. Of the two groups, Singletails are the most hardy and can overwinter in an outside pond. Only the familiar metallic-looking, orange-red fishes can be regarded as anywhere near a natural species as the other colour forms are aquarium-developed.

Similarly, Twintails are not fishes that are naturally-occurring, as their physical features have been developed over many years in the aquarium and pond by selective breeding programmes. Twintails are more delicate, both in form and constitution; they require special care and attention, extra-clean water conditions and, if kept outdoors, must be brought back indoors before winter sets in.

2
GOLDFISH ANATOMY

Apart from the exaggerated physical characteristics bred into the more Fancy Varieties, the anatomy of the Goldfish conforms to that structure found in other fishes.

Figure 4. Familiarising yourself with the main external features of the fish, as indicated below, will enable you to spot any variety's identifying characteristics, and understand better how a fish functions. Sizes shown in fish books usually refer to the Standard Length (true body length) rather than the Total Length. The latter will include any long flowing fins — which might not necessarily be complete at the time of measuring!

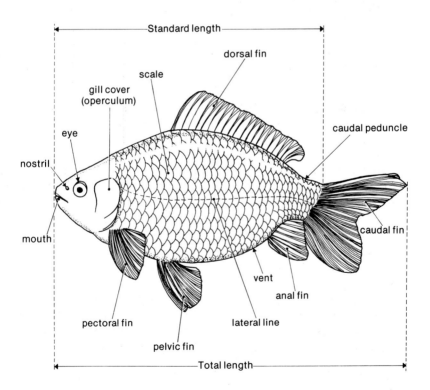

FINS

There are seven fins – three single ones and two pairs. The single fins, the *dorsal, anal* and *caudal* are used mainly for stability and propulsion. The paired fins, the *pectoral* and *pelvic* (also known as the *ventral* fins) are used for manoeuvring (vertically and laterally) and for braking the forward motion.

SCALES

Most fish are covered with a protective layer of hard scales over their skin. In addition to protection, scales also give the fish extra streamlining and help it to slip through the water more efficiently.

Fishkeeping would be in a sad state if it was not for the colours and shine of the fishes and the Goldfish does more than most to play its part in this attraction. Goldfishes can be divided into three distinct groups – *metallic, nacreous* and *matt* – depending on their 'shininess'. Many fishkeepers call these 'scale-groups' but it is not the scales themselves which are transparent, that determine the group but how much reflective material *(guanin)* is present beneath the skin.

In the *metallic* fishes, there is a large amount of guanin. The Common Goldfish is a good example of a highly metallic red-orange fish. The *nacreous* fishes have a smaller amount of guanin and this gives the scales a 'mother-of-pearl' lustre. *Matt* fishes have a dull finish due to a complete lack of guanin.

COLOURS

Pigmentation within Goldfishes allows many colours to be seen, particularly in nacreous and matt types, where the absence, or limited amount, of guanin beneath the skin results in multi-coloured fishes; blue, violet, black, orange and yellow are quite common colours. Metallic fishes are usually either red/orange or white/silver.

RESPIRATORY ORGANS

Dissolved oxygen is extracted from the water by the *gills*. These delicate membranes are located on each side of the head and are protected by an external bony flap known as the *gill-cover* or *operculum*. To breathe, a fish inhales water into its mouth, which it then shuts, forcing out the water through the opening behind the gill-cover, thus passing it over the gills as it does so.

SENSORY ORGANS

Fishes share the same five senses as Man but depend on them to different degrees. Their sense of *hearing*, for example, may be less acute and they rely more on their lateral-line systems which sense vibrations in the water. *Taste* may be experienced through taste cells on the fish's skin, as well as where normally expected, in the mouth. The sense of *smell* is highly developed but the nostrils are used for this purpose only, playing no part in *respiration* at all. The senses of *touch* and *sight* function in the normal way.

LATERAL-LINE SYSTEM

A horizontal row of pierced scales along the fish's flanks (the *lateral-line*), allows the fish's nervous system to communicate directly with the outside environment (i.e. the water). Any vibration in the water, made for instance by another passing fish, wriggling live foods or by water currents, can be detected. This sense can be a great help in dimly-lit water or even in complete darkness.

3
SELECTING A TANK
FOR YOUR GOLDFISHES

Right at the outset, please dismiss any idea of keeping Goldfishes in a bowl. A bowl is quite unsuitable for many reasons: it will not support very many fishes; it does not provide the fish with enough swimming space; it needs to be cleaned out at least once a week; and it doesn't even look very natural! It is far better to keep Goldfishes in a proper aquarium, where everything can be done to ensure that the fishes' comfort and well-being are not neglected. But having made this point, not just any tank will do; it should be of the correct proportions.

Tank design and construction are of more importance to you than the fishes and will be dealt with later in this chapter.

THE CORRECT SIZE
Coldwater fishkeepers have a couple of slight advantages over their tropical-fishkeeping friends; their aquariums need no heating and the cooler water in their tanks holds more dissolved oxygen. Despite these two apparent merits, the aquarium for coldwater fish still needs to be larger than that for tropical fishes or, to put it another way, not as many coldwater fishes as tropical ones can be kept in a given tank capacity. The main factor affecting the size of tank for any fish is adequate provision for the supply of oxygen to, and the removal of carbon dioxide from, the aquarium water.

Fishes extract dissolved oxygen from the aquarium water through their gills and, as a result of the respiration process, carbon dioxide and water are expelled through the gills. Ammonia, a by-product of protein metabolism, may also be released via the gills.

For the continuing support of the fishes, it is vital that the dissolved oxygen content of the water is kept as high as possible and that the level of carbon dioxide is kept as low as possible. The supply and discharge of gases can only occur at the interface between the water and the atmosphere; in the case of the aquarium (or any body of water), this interface is the water surface.

To ensure that the oxygen supply is continuously replenished,

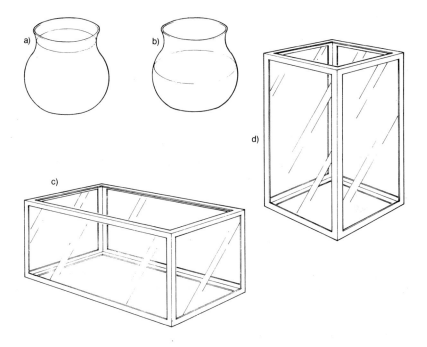

Figure 5. The number of fishes you can keep depends on the area of water surface available through which oxygen can be absorbed into the water. A completely filled bowl (a) has a small surface area; only filling it half-full (b) improves the situation but gives the fish less room to swim! The two rectangular tanks (c and d) will both hold the same amount of water (swimming room) but by using the tank horizontally (c) a much larger water surface area is obtained. This tank will hold the most fish.

it is obvious that the larger the surface area of water presented to the atmosphere the better. (Apart from the added luxury of the fishes having more room to swim about in, the actual depth of water in an aquarium has little bearing on the number of fishes that the aquarium will support.)

The diffusion of carbon dioxide from the water surface occurs only slowly, but there are ways in which it can be accelerated. Alternatively the carbon dioxide can be removed by other means, e.g. *aeration* (p. 26) and *photosynthesis* (p. 29).

As a rough guide, you should allow 24 in² of water surface area for every inch of fish body length. (When measuring the fish's body do not include the tail, just measure from the tip of the nose to where

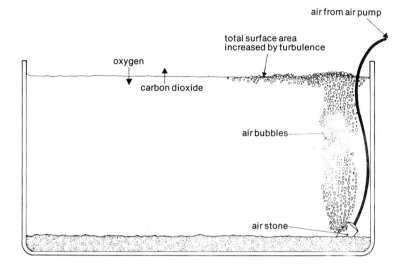

Figure 6. Even if the water surface area is adequate, the absorption rate of oxygen into the water (and the expellation of carbon dioxide from it) can be increased by using an air stone to create turbulence at the water surface.

the tail joins on to the body.) In metric measurements, this is equivalent to 60 cm^2 for every centimetre of fish body length.

In order for the aquarium to suit all requirements (yours as well as the fishes'), it is recommended that a tank of not less than 36 in long by 12 in front to back by 12 in deep is used. This will allow you to have a reasonable number of fishes and, because of its size, water conditions will remain more stable and less likely to fluctuate in temperature. Smaller tanks can be used for quarantine purposes, perhaps a hospital or breeding tank, but for general fishkeeping they generally turn out to need a little more attention than larger tanks if they are to be kept in tip-top condition.

If we examine our theoretical, correct-sized tank we will find that it has a water surface area of 432 in^2 (length 36 in × width 12 in). Dividing this by 24 (in^2), we find that a total of 18 in of fish body length can be accommodated in the tank. You cannot take such calculations too literally, as six fishes, each 3 in long, would obviously be more comfortable in the tank than one single 18-in long fish, which would have a job to even turn around!

Translated into approximate metric units, and taking a tank 100

18

cm long by 30 cm wide, the number of 1-cm long fishes which the tank could hold would be fifty ($100 \times 30 \div 60$). Again five 10-cm fishes would be more comfortable than one 50-cm monster!

TANK VOLUMES, WEIGHTS AND FISH CAPACITIES

Table 1 provides a quick guide to the more commonly-used sizes of aquaria. Use it to find out how much water the tank of your choice holds, how much it weighs (just with water alone, never mind the gravel and rocks!) and how many fish it will hold.

Table 1. *Tank dimensions and related features*

Dimensions h x w x d in (cm)	Volume Gallons UK (US) (litres)	Weight Freshwater lb (kg)	Fish Total length in (cm)
*18 x 10 x 10 (45 x 25 x 25)	6 (7) (28.1)	60 (28.1)	7 (18)
**24 x 12 x 12 (60 x 30 x 30)	12 (14) (54)	120 (54)	12 (30)
**24 x 12 x 15 (60 x 30 x 38)	15 (18) (68.4)	150 (68.4)	12 (30)
36 x 12 x 15 (90 x 30 x 38)	23 (27) (102.6)	230 (102.6)	18 (45)
48 x 12 x 15 (120 x 30 x 38)	30 (36) (136.8)	300 (136.8)	24 (60)

*Unsuitable for general fishkeeping but could be useful as a hospital tank, or for quarantine purposes.
**These aquariums have the same surface area although of differing total volumes, and can only support the same number of fishes.

TYPES OF TANK

By now, the reasons for the unsuitability of the Goldfish bowl will have become apparent; the maximum surface area of any bowl is provided when the water level reaches the bowl's widest part – halfway up – so in order to get the maximum exchange of gases, the fishes' swimming space must automatically be restricted. Add to these drawbacks, the fact that the glass bowl usually gives a distorted view of the fishes and you will quickly come to the conclusion that the bowl's only practical virtue is that it holds water!

The modern aquarium tank will more than likely be one of two types; either a one-piece of moulded acrylic plastic or an all-glass

19

construction. Tanks made using the older method of glass panes set in a metal frame (which was prone to rust sooner or later) are no longer commonly available.

One-piece tanks are now a much better proposition than they were some years ago; the clarity of the plastic is better and little discolouration occurs. You still need to exercise caution when cleaning the front, to avoid scratching the plastic, and sometimes the plastic hoods are not too well-designed for use with hot-running tungsten lamps (p. 51). The only reservation about their use is that they may not be available in the larger sizes necessary for coldwater-fishkeeping.

Since the introduction of modern adhesives and sealing materials, it is now possible to make a tank from five pieces of glass simply stuck together to form a watertight box. This facility immediately allows you to make a tank of just the right dimensions to suit the chosen location. However, standard sizes of tanks are commercially available. In Europe, tanks are generally referred to by their dimensions, whereas it is quite common for American fishkeepers to refer to their tanks by the number of gallons which they hold.

SITING OF THE TANK

From Table 1, you will see that a fully-filled tank, even one of modest proportions, is very heavy, so serious consideration must be given to the suitability of any proposed site for the aquarium. The foundation for any aquarium must be firm and level; specially-designed stands are available, either of iron or incorporated into the design of a piece of furniture. It is also important that the weight of the aquarium is distributed evenly, both on the surface of the stand and on the floor. The former can be achieved by resting a slab of expanded polystyrene (cut to the size of the aquarium base) on the stand before the tank is placed in position; this will cushion out any unevenness and prevent stresses being set up which might result in a cracked glass panel. The aquarium stand itself should rest so that the weight is distributed across the floor joists, and the legs of the stand (particularly those made of iron) should have pads beneath them to avoid damage to carpets.

Aquaria can also be incorporated into bookshelves, but they should not be mounted too high. Apart from being difficult to see into (and to maintain), such a location will result in a high centre of gravity for the bookcase, increasing the danger of it toppling over.

For the same reason, the bookshelves, especially those below the tank, should be kept full of books to maintain stability.

Weight is not the only factor to take into consideration when choosing a site. The aquarium should not be situated where it will be exposed to variations in temperature. For this reason, a window location is bad, especially if it is one that receives a fair amount of direct sunshine. Too much sunshine will a) cause excessive growths of green algae and b) raise the water temperature uncontrollably. A fireside location, or a radiator in close proximity to the aquarium will also affect the water temperature. It is best to site the aquarium in a position where it cannot be disturbed and where it only receives a little direct daylight; in this way, the amount of light reaching the aquarium can easily be controlled.

A location near to an electrical power outlet is to be preferred, as the aquarium will require power to work the lighting and filtration equipment and it is unwise to have great lengths of cable lying about. There should also be enough space left above and below the aquarium for ease of maintenance and storage of associated equipment.

These are the reasons why most aquaria are situated in an otherwise unused alcove; they are out of the way, unlikely to be affected by temperature-raising, algae-encouraging, direct sunlight and make a self-contained fishkeeping area, which also gives the room an interesting feature.

4
WATER

Despite 'Nature's own' generally being regarded as the best, the majority of fishkeepers do not have ready access to bodies of fresh water; neither does water collected naturally always quite fit the bill. Water is the fishes' equivalent to the atmosphere that we breathe, and we should ensure that it is 'breathable' to them at all times.

Fortunately, the Goldfish is very tolerant in respect of the water in which it is kept, and most are kept in water from the domestic supply. There is no reason to worry about the quality of water from the tap, providing that one or two precautions are taken.

The domestic water supply is quite heavily filtered and treated by the water engineers to be fit for human consumption; some of the substances added may not always be harmless to fishes. The main additive is chlorine and this can be dispersed from the water in two ways: a) if water is transported to the aquarium by bucket rather than a direct hosepipe, much of the chlorine can be driven out from the water by filling the bucket vigorously; b) once the aquarium has been filled, a period of strong aeration will drive off any chlorine remaining in the water within the next 24 – 48 hours. There are proprietary additives available from your aquatic dealer which will precipitate heavy metals, such as copper and zinc, from the water, but many fishkeepers prefer not to add still more chemicals to the water.

Principal poisons affecting the water are metals and water that has been standing in copper pipework for any length of time (particularly if the pipework is new) should not be used for the aquarium. It is best to run off any water that has been standing in the pipe before filling the aquarium.

If you accept that most fishkeepers live in towns, there is every chance that any rainwater collected for use in the aquarium will be polluted to some extent by absorbing toxic substances as it falls through the atmosphere. The alternative of collecting fresh water from a natural source, such as a country river or stream, is beyond practicability for most people.

Rainwater can be used, although it is likely to be of a far different composition to tap water; it should be collected from a clean surface, through plastic guttering, into plastic containers. It is advisable not to collect all the water in any period of rainfall, but to let the first few minutes of constant rain wash the dust and dirt off the roof before collecting the rest.

WATER QUALITY

You should be aware of the various qualities of water, although you may never need to actually alter the water composition.

Water can be either acid or alkaline and hard or soft. Many fishkeepers are aware of these two quite different qualities, although there may be some confusion at times between them.

The pH of water

The acidity or alkalinity of water depends on what substances are absorbed by the water, either as it falls through the atmosphere or as it seeps through the earth on its way to the river and, eventually, the sea. It is measured on a logarithmic scale known as the *pH Scale*. This scale ranges from 0 (strongest acid) to 14 (strongest alkali); the range that concerns fishkeepers is around pH 6.6 – 7.5. You will notice that this is very near to the mid-point in the pH range; this point (pH 7) is known as the neutral point where water is neither acid nor alkaline.

Water from the tap is generally around pH 7.2 – 7.5. Rainwater is usually much more acidic and may have a pH of around 6.5. pH can be determined by the use of *pH Test Kits*. These are simple to use and consist of colour-indicating reagents which are added to a sample of the aquarium water; the resulting colour is compared with a standard colour chart which indicates the pH.

Hardness

Water hardness is due to dissolved materials, mainly bicarbonates and sulphates of calcium and magnesium salts. Hardness of water is nothing strange to us, as everyone is aware of the different amounts of soap required to make the same amount of lather, on moving from one area of water hardness to another. The bicarbonates are responsible for *temporary hardness* (which can be removed by boiling), but *permanent hardness,* caused by sulphates, can only be removed by a chemical process.

Again, like pH, water hardness can be determined by the use of a test kit, where a reagent causes a colour change to occur in a sample of aquarium water. In this case, the amount of reagent used to effect the colour change is an indication of the water's hardness figure.

Hardness can be reduced quite simply by dilution. If a volume of soft water (rain water or distilled water) is added to the same volume of hard water, the resulting overall hardness will be a simple arithmetic average of the two hardnesses.

EFFECT OF DIFFERING WATER QUALITIES

Changes in water quality affect the fishes in many ways; their eyes may become cloudy or there may be an excessive amount of mucus produced on the skin; colours may become enhanced or dulled; eggs may not develop properly and may disintegrate.

New fishkeepers often worry about whether fishes obtained outside their immediate locality will survive a transfer to their own aquarium. If, say, the aquatic dealer is only a few miles away, there is every chance that the fishes are being kept in water very similar to that from your own supply. It is only when fishes are obtained from water conditions that are known, or suspected, to be different that there may be problems.

You should never move a fish from one type of water straight into water that is known to be of a different quality as it will be put under an enormous stress. The fish should be acclimatised gradually to any new water. This can be accomplished easily by gradually replacing part of the fish's existing water with some of the new water until, over a reasonably long period of time, the water has been changed completely to the new quality.

MAINTAINING WATER QUALITY

You should be very careful what you put into the aquarium as it is quite easy to upset the water conditions. Many rocks are unsuitable because of their metallic or soluble material content. Similarly, poisons or coloured dyes in prefabricated aquarium decorations may leach out into the water. Gravel dredged from the seashore has a high content of seashell fragments that will also affect the water composition. Tree roots and other woods used for decoration, unless rendered safe, will release tannins into the water and make it discoloured and acidic.

The use of filters to clean the water is described in Chapter 8 and regular partial changes of water will ensure that your fishes remain healthy.

5
AERATION

In the previous chapter, it was mentioned that vigorous agitation of the water helped to disperse gases such as chlorine; even earlier (p. 18), the importance of assisting the access of oxygen into the water and the expulsion of carbon dioxide from it was discussed.

The means of agitating the water is provided by *aeration*. In essence, compressed air is fed into the aquarium via a submerged porous block and the resulting stream of air bubbles creates a current of water around the aquarium.

As the water is continually being turned over, a greater area of water is brought into contact with the atmosphere and oxygen can enter into the water much more freely. Goldfish appreciate well-oxygenated water.

Similarly, there is added opportunity for carbon dioxide to escape. The practical side-effect of this aeration is effectively to increase

Figure 7. An air stone creates water circulation and helps to equalize the temperature throughout the aquarium. It also brings water from the lower levels to the top ensuring that there are no pockets of stale water.

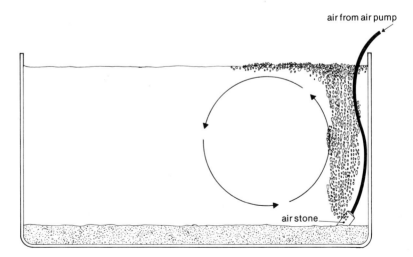

air from air pump

air stone

the water surface area and, as you learned earlier, a larger surface area means only one thing to a fishkeeper – more fish in the tank!

Unfortunately, you don't get anything for nothing and, along with this apparent bonus, there comes a danger: should the air supply fail, the aquarium will revert to its normal fish-holding capacity as calculated without aeration. So, if you have 'overstocked' your aquarium, there is a danger of your fishes becoming distressed, either through a shortage of oxygen (unlikely) but, more probably, through a build-up of carbon dioxide, especially during periods of warm weather. Don't use aeration as an excuse to keep more fish but do, by all means, use it to make the fishes' lives more comfortable. You can also make good use of the air from the air pump to operate a filter system, a Brine-Shrimp-hatching system or an air-operated sediment-remover.

AIR PUMPS AND THEIR CARE

Air pumps may be of two types, vibrator-diaphragm or rotary-driven piston/vane pumps.

Of the two, vibrator pumps are commonest, with many models, ranging from the cheap and noisy to the very expensive and relatively quiet. Even the most modest vibrator pump will produce enough air for both an air stone and a filtration system, and the larger models are quite capable of satisfying the needs of a multi-tank fish-house. Rotary-driven, piston or vane pumps produce much larger quantities of air and are really very highly engineered pieces of equipment; some people are fascinated just by their mechanical action alone!

Maintenance of pumps is no problem, diaphragm replacement is simple and straightforward – but do remember to *switch off the electrical supply first.* Piston pumps usually only need a little regular lubrication to ensure constant efficiency. The air being pumped into the aquarium should be clean; air can be contaminated by many things – tobacco smoke, any aerosols, paint fumes, dust, perfumes to name but a few. Remember that polluted air is being pumped into the aquarium for 24 hours a day and take steps to filter it. This can be done quite easily: there is usually a felt air filter built into the base of most vibrator pumps. This should be removed periodically for cleaning. Well-lubricated piston pumps will produce oily air, and this oil should be filtered out (through a wad of cotton-wool) before the air reaches the aquarium.

27

The pump should be protected against its main enemy, water. If the pump is situated below the aquarium, on a convenient shelf, there is a possibility that, if the pump stops (or is switched off), water will siphon out of the aquarium and back down the air line, into the pump, thus causing a short circuit when the electricity is switched on again. To prevent this, it is advisable to site the pump above the aquarium water level if possible or, failing this, to connect a one-way valve into the air supply.

6

AQUARIUM PLANTS

To many fishkeepers, aquarium plants provide as much interest and attraction as do the fishes, and there is the added bonus that aquarium plants do much more than just beautify.

USES OF PLANTS

In the aquarium, the plants, like the fishes, respire all the time and, in so doing, use up oxygen and give out carbon dioxide and water. However, in the presence of light, plants produce their own food stocks from carbon dioxide and water in a process called *photosynthesis*. The by-products of this are oxygen and water. The net effect, during the periods when the aquarium is illuminated (by electric light or sunlight), is a reduction in the amount of carbon dioxide in the water and an increase in the amount of oxygen. Thus, plants perform a most important service for the aquarium.

Figure 8. When the aquarium is lit, plants produce excess oxygen and take in carbon dioxide during the photosynthesis process. At night this process seemingly goes into reverse, the plants taking in oxygen and giving off carbon dioxide in the same way as the fishes' normal respiration pattern.

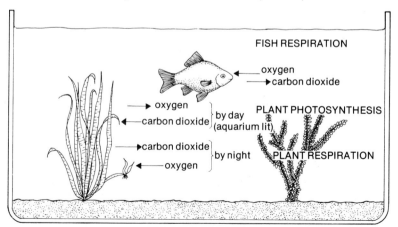

Additionally, plants bring welcome shade to the fishes and provide retreats and refuges within their stems and leaves. Many fishes make use of plants as spawning sites during the breeding period and some fishes will browse upon the softer-leaved varieties.

TYPES OF PLANTS

Although the choice of plants for the coldwater aquarium is not as large as for tropical aquaria, the plants come in many shapes and sizes, leaf-shapes and colours. They may be rooted in the aquarium gravel or allowed to float freely in the water or upon its surface. Not all the plants which are rooted in the gravel feed through their roots; many obtain nourishment directly through their leaves and merely use their roots to anchor them into place. Other species use their roots to stick themselves to rocks or submerged logs.

Fishkeepers usually classify plants into three broad groups – those which root in the gravel, those which float freely and those species which provide new plants from easily-rooted cuttings or individual, severed leaves.

USING PLANTS

Fast-growing rooted species include the grass-like plants and these make excellent background plants. Some grow quite tall and their leaves will trail over the water surface to provide shade. Slower-growing plants can be featured as 'specimen' plants and should be set out in a prominent area of the aquarium where their individual beauty can be easily appreciated.

Bushy plants are best used to fill space, particularly corners and between rocks. Although rooted in clumps when established in the aquarium, these plants are generally sold as bunches of cuttings by the aquatic dealer. Cuttings can be taken from any fine-leaved plant and weighted and re-rooted in the gravel to make extra new plants. The effect of taking cuttings will be to make the parent plant develop side shoots, with the result that the plant becomes bushier.

Floating plants are useful as shading plants, but only if they are kept under control, for they tend to spread across the surface of the water very quickly and prevent the light reaching the rest of the plants. Species that hang or float freely in the water may also need thinning out but the surplus can be utilised in the breeding tank as spawning media rather than being simply thrown out.

The planting of the aquarium is very much a subjective affair and you will want to do your own thing in this respect. Planting and layout hints are given in Chapter 10.

PLANT SPECIES

Sagittaria and *Vallisneria* are two similar-looking plants, although they belong to different families, and are widely used in both tropical and cold freshwater aquaria; you should make sure that the species is acclimatised for the particular type of aquarium in which you intend to use it.

The two genera are ideal for backgrounds, effectively hiding the walls of the aquarium. Occasionally you will find that these two plants will not get on together in the same aquarium, and it will then be a case of deciding which one to discard in order to concentrate on the other. Both reproduce by sending out runners and the new plants can be severed from the parent plants as soon as they have become established with a few leaves.

Plants with different leaf forms show up well against the background of the narrow leaves of the previous species. *Bacopa caroliniana* and *Ludwigia repens* are two plants with fleshy leaves growing in pairs on opposite sides of the plant stem. *Ludwigia* leaves often have reddish undersides.

Propagation of both species is by cuttings, but this does not result in the donor plant becoming bushier; in order to have a clump of these species, it is necessary to plant several specimens close together.

Potamogeton crispus is generally thought of as a pond plant, but enterprising fishkeepers may find that it takes to aquarium life just as well. Propagation is by cuttings.

A pleasing effect can be obtained by siting small plants in the gravel against the vertical front faces of rocks, rather than merely placing plants out in the open swimming space. *Acorus* and *Eleocharis* are two such plants. *Acorus* is generally known as the Dwarf Japanese Rush whilst there is no doubt as to the aptness of the common name for *Eleocharis* – Hairgrass.

Figure 9 (Overleaf). Use fast-growing plants around the edges and back to form a background; bushy plants fill out the corners and are ideal as a spawning medium; small plants are best used as foreground coverings. Floating plants give welcome shade and hiding places for young fishes.

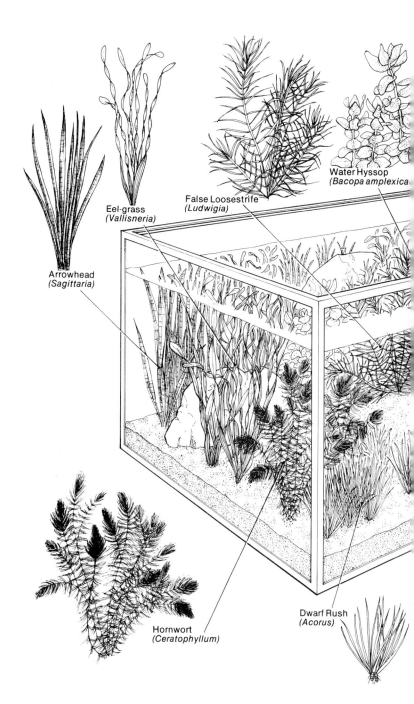

Arrowhead
(Sagittaria)

Eel-grass
(Vallisneria)

False Loosestrife
(Ludwigia)

Water Hyssop
(Bacopa amplexica

Hornwort
(Ceratophyllum)

Dwarf Rush
(Acorus)

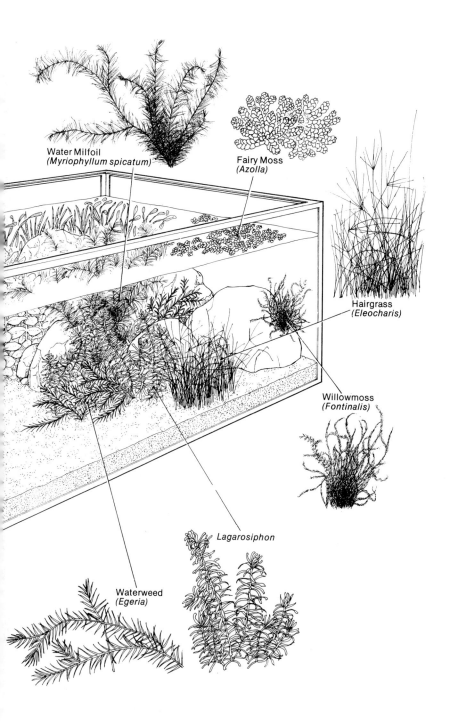

Water Milfoil
(Myriophyllum spicatum)

Fairy Moss
(Azolla)

Hairgrass
(Eleocharis)

Willowmoss
(Fontinalis)

Lagarosiphon

Waterweed
(Egeria)

Acorus may eventually die off after a long period of being submerged for it is a bog or marsh plant by nature. *Eleocharis* makes a very pleasing feature, particularly in the front corners of a tall tank, where the needle-shaped leaves form a very attractive framing for the underwater scene. Propagation of both species is by division of the root stock or rhizome.

Masses of fine-leaved plants in midwater provide spawning sites for fishes, food for others and are often a feature of coldwater aquaria and outside ponds. *Egeria densa, Elodea canadensis* (Canadian Pondweed), *Ceratophyllum demersum* (Hornwort), *Lagarosiphon major* (often confused with, and sold as, *Elodea crispa*) and *Myriophyllum spicatum* (Milfoil) are all established favourites. Most are fast growers and will provide any amount of new stock from cuttings which can be weighted down to re-root in the gravel. These plants should not be allowed to become choked with algae or dirt; this means that you have to keep the water well filtered and watch closely the amount of light that you allow into the aquarium. Should the fishes take advantage of these plants as a spawning medium, it is a simple matter to transfer clumps of the egg-laden plants to another tank for hatching.

Fontinalis antipyretica (Willow Moss) is a member of the Fern family and anchors itself to any submerged object, rather than rooting in the gravel. Like the previous species, it is an excellent spawning medium and care should be taken to protect it from algae and detritus; a quick rinse under running water will usually clean it up again quite satisfactorily.

To some fishkeepers, floating plants have a charm of their own; to others, they are more trouble than they're worth! Because of their position in the tank (right up under the aquarium lights), they do grow very quickly and will turn any initial welcoming shade they bring into complete darkness if they are allowed to take over the entire water surface. Propagation is hardly ever a problem – just try to stop them! *Azolla caroliniana* (Fairy Moss), *Lemna minor* (Duckweed) and *Riccia fluitans* (Crystalwort) are typical floating plants; the reddish-tinged *Azolla* and the delicately-structured, semi-submerged *Riccia* are more attractive than the Duckweed.

SOURCES OF PLANTS

The majority of aquarium plants are usually obtainable without difficulty from your aquatic dealer or some of the larger nursery

34

garden centres which may specialise in water garden plants. You can, of course, collect some species yourself from a local stream or river; costs are small and stocks can be easily replaced but there is a danger of introducing predacious insect larvae, snails' eggs and even disease into the aquarium. Any plants collected from the wild should be thoroughly inspected for unwelcome guests before introducing them into the aquarium.

7

LIGHTING

One obvious purpose of having light entering the aquarium is so that the fishkeeper can see the fishes, but light fulfils much more important purposes than that. Light stimulates life and activity in the aquarium; it also provides the energy by which the plants photosynthesise their food stocks, utilising the carbon dioxide in the water and releasing oxygen.

PROVISION OF CORRECT AMOUNT OF LIGHT

If the aquarium is sited as recommended, the fishkeeper will have complete control of the amount of light falling into the aquarium. This is most critical as both too little and too much can cause problems. The main criterion governing the amount of light is the wellbeing of the aquarium plants. Plants require a certain minimum level of light in order to thrive, below this level they appear to mark time and gradually fade away. Conversely, plants cannot make use of too much light and any excess above their requirements is not only wasted (and expensive), but may encourage the growth of green algae.

For optimum plant growth, the aquarium should be lit for 10-15 hours each day. The strength of the illumination should be quite bright for the majority of this period, but the brightness can be reduced to a more comfortable viewing level during the evening, when most of one's 'fish-watching' is done.

The actual strength and duration of the light is best arrived at by trial and error, but a starting point would be to allow either 40 watts of tungsten lighting or 10 watts of fluorescent lighting per 12 in (30 cm) length of tank. These figures should be increased a little for tanks with a water depth in excess of 18 in (45 cm).

Too much light usually results in the excessive growth of green algae; the remedy is either to reduce the strength or duration of illumination or to utilise the light's energy more fully by adding more plants to crowd out the algae. Too little light is indicated by the plants not growing at all, or appearing very 'leggy' and thin. If you are already lighting the aquarium for the suggested period then the next thing to do is increase the lamp's brightness.

One problem is that, if you try to cultivate too many different species of plants, you will eventually find that the lighting levels will not suit all the plants as some need brighter or dimmer lighting than others. Some shade can be provided in the aquarium by the use of plants with long leaves which trail across the water surface; floating species can also be used, although these usually become quite rampant in a very short space of time unless thinned out continually. Another solution is to grow only species requiring the same lighting conditions. (Another reason for apparent incompatibility amongst plants is that no single set of water conditions will suit all plants.)

TYPES OF LIGHTING
Unless you have installed your aquarium where it receives direct, but controllable, amounts of natural light, the only other practicable alternative is electric light. Lamps can be either incandescent or fluorescent types. It is quite normal to use either quite separately

Figure 10. You can fit either tungsten or fluorescent lighting (or a combination of both) in the normal aquarium hood/reflector. Some modern designs have a section especially built in to accommodate the starting gear for the fluorescent tubes.

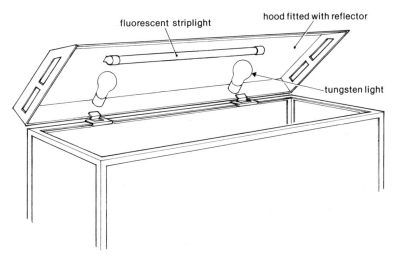

fluorescent striplight

hood fitted with reflector

tungsten light

37

or to have a combination of the two each with its own independent switch to allow complete control.

Both types have their merits and disadvantages and, in the long run, there is probably not much actual difference between them providing you are satisfied with the end result.

Incandescent lamps are cheaper to buy, easier to install but run hotter, cost more to operate, can heat up the surface layers of the water and may well have a short lamp-life in the overheated confines of the aquarium hood. (Make sure the hood has sufficient ventilation holes in it.)

Fluorescent lamps are cheaper to run but more complicated to install and more expensive to buy; they run cool, give out an even spread of light and have a longer lamp-life. There are also lamps especially designed to assist plant growth and different 'colours' from which to choose.

CARE OF EQUIPMENT

The lamps in the aquarium hood are very vulnerable to damage from water or damp. The lamp fittings should be waterproof and safeguarded against either direct splashes or condensation by the use of a cover-glass fitted on the tank; this will also protect the leaves of any floating plant against scorch damage from the heat of the lamps.

Keep the reflector/hood and cover-glass spotlessly clean, so that all the available light is not only efficiently directed down into the aquarium, but also reaches the plants at full strength and is not restricted by a dirty cover-glass.

A final point: some fishes are easily shocked by the sudden switching on or off of the aquarium lights. You can minimise this risk by leaving the room lights burning for a few minutes after switching off the aquarium at night, and by switching them on for a few minutes on dark mornings before switching on the aquarium lights.

8
FILTRATION

The water in the aquarium will become contaminated and dirty and must be kept clean. Regular partial water changes will do this to some extent, but the use of efficient filtration systems will not only provide a means of constant cleansing but will also help to keep the water oxygenated at the same time. Partial water changes should not be neglected, however, even if an efficient filter is used.

Goldfishes are foraging fishes and they do a lot of rummaging about in the aquarium gravel, which naturally produces quite a lot of sediment which floats in suspension in the water and settles on plants, generally making the aquarium look dirty. A filter will strain out the suspended matter and help to keep the water clean. Filters will also remove dissolved waste products if the correct filter medium is used.

TYPES OF FILTERS

There are three main types of filters: mechanical, chemical and biological. The first two types are usually combined in one design and the first and third types combined in another.

Mechanical and chemical filters

The basic working principle of these filters is to draw water from the aquarium, pass it through a cleansing medium and return the cleaned water to the aquarium. Filters may be of internal or external design and be operated either by air (from the air pump) or by small electrically-driven impellers.

Impeller-driven filters are more suitable for Goldfish aquaria as they have a larger throughput of water and, consequently, can be used to better effect on larger (and dirtier) tanks. The choice of design is quite large, but one advantage the external types have over internal models is that you do not need to disturb the aquarium in any way when cleaning the filter medium.

Air-operated mechanical and chemical filters are best used for

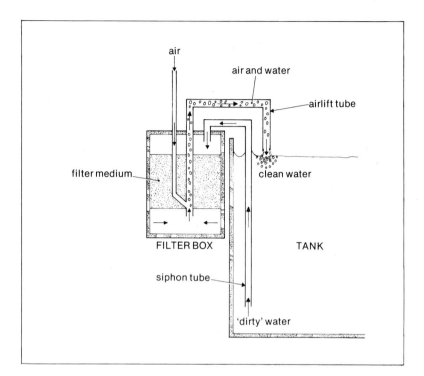

Figure 11. Dirty aquarium water is fed into the outside filter box by a siphon tube which automatically stops when the filter box is full of water. The water flows down through the filter medium and clean water is returned to the aquarium by way of the airlift tube. More powerful filters are recommended for Goldfish aquariums and these have the water returned by an electric impeller rather than a simple airlift.

smaller tanks, such as those used for tropical species, or, where coldwater species are concerned, for special purposes, such as fry-raising or hospitalisation.

Filter media usually consist of a manmade fibrous substance, such as *nylon floss;* this will trap any suspended sediment in the water as it passes through the filter body and it can be washed through and re-used a few times. Some pre-filter medium is advised to strain out the larger particles and thus prevent the floss from becoming clogged too rapidly; there is a substance which looks like small pieces of macaroni available from most aquatic stores which works admirably in this respect – the 'macaroni' is, in fact, sections of small ceramic pipe.

Do not be tempted to use either cotton-wool or glass-wool; the former will clog up in no time at all and the latter may well release small slivers of glass fibre into the aquarium water and damage the delicate gill membranes of the fishes, as they take in water to pass over their gills.

Another form of filter medium, used in conjunction with nylon floss is *activated carbon,* which adsorbs dissolved fishes' waste products from the water. Filters containing activated carbon should be turned off (or the carbon removed) when treating diseases in the aquarium, as the carbon will adsorb the medication. It is usual practice to sandwich a layer of activated carbon between two layers of nylon floss to prevent it being drawn into the aquarium with the returning clean water.

Care should be exercised when fitting any external filters. Make sure all the water-carrying pipes are securely fixed otherwise the power filter will pump the liquid contents of your aquarium onto the floor just as efficiently!

Clean, or renew, the filter medium regularly, a slowing down of the water rate from a filter indicates that it is becoming clogged. If you mount an external filter on the aquarium so that it is out of sight, make sure it is not out of mind.

BIOLOGICAL FILTERS

There are no moving parts to these filters and they are practically invisible when installed in the aquarium.

Biological filters work in a totally different way to mechanical and chemical filters; mechanical filtration does occur to some extent during their operation but it does not form the major part of their operating principle.

Biological filtration makes use of the fact that some bacteria (*Nitrosomonas* and *Nitrobacter*) break down ammonia, nitrite and other toxic nitrogenous products into less harmful substances. To do this, the bacteria must have well-oxygenated conditions and a large surface area on which to live. These conditions can be arranged quite easily in the aquarium and the ideal place is in the aquarium gravel.

Water is pumped, or drawn, through the gravel by means of a filter-type air lift, or impeller, and the bacteria colonise the surface area of each grain of gravel. As long as the water flow is continuous, the bacteria thrive and do their job; if the water flow stops due to

41

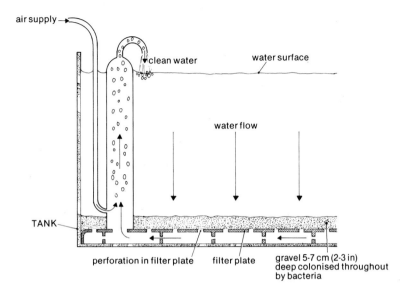

air supply →

clean water

water surface

water flow

TANK

perforation in filter plate   filter plate   gravel 5-7 cm (2-3 in) deep colonised throughout by bacteria

Figure 12. Water is drawn down through the gravel and back to the top of the aquarium by an airlift tube. (An electric impeller can be fitted to increase the water flow if required.) The bacteria in the gravel bed convert dangerous ammonia-based compounds into less harmful substances. NEVER SWITCH OFF THE AIR SUPPLY TO SUCH A FILTER.

an air pump failure, or switch off, the bacteria die and start polluting the tank. WARNING: *Never turn off the air supply or water flow, to a biological filter.*

The filter plate should be protected from exposure by the rummaging fishes by concealing a nylon mesh within the gravel layer (p. 48).

Because the activities of Goldfishes always result in a certain amount of suspended material in the water, biological filtration alone may not be enough to keep the water clean. An efficient external filter should also be used and it is possible to use the external mechanical filter to pump cleaned water through the biological filter in the reverse direction to that normally used, i.e. up through the gravel instead of downwards.

9
AQUARIUM DECORATION

Two advantages that the indoor aquarium has over the outside pond is that the fish can not only be seen at all times, but are also visible from almost their own viewpoint within their environment. This being the case, it is only natural that the fishkeeper should prefer his or her aquarium to look like a natural underwater scene and not just a water-filled box. Apart from this, perhaps selfish, but nevertheless aesthetic, need of the fishkeeper, there are also other very good reasons why the aquarium should be furnished and these are described below.

SECURITY FOR THE FISHES

Fishes living in open waters are usually fast-swimming predators or shoaling fishes, well able to look after themselves. Other species would be distinctly nervous in such unprotected areas. Similarly, fishes swimming over a plain- or light-coloured base (one not covered up by gravel, for example) will show up more clearly to any predators above, whilst to the viewer, seeing them from the side, their colours appear faded or washed-out.

Fishes also appreciate some shade and shelter, places where they can relax or even hide from other species if necessary. Such places can be provided by the plants and rockwork in the aquarium. You need not worry too much about the creation of caves or grottoes in the Goldfish aquarium as the fishes are not territorially minded, nor as secretive as some of the tropical fishes; however, Goldfishes will appreciate a planted aquarium and they are great rummagers in the gravel.

BREEDING AIDS FOR FISHES

Plants, described more fully elsewhere, will also provide spawning sites for fishes. Fine-leaved plants act as very efficient egg-collectors and may be used to good effect by spawning Goldfishes, although the fishes may also look upon plants as food from time to time.

Fortunately, plants likely to be affected, such as *Ceratophyllum,* *Egeria,* and *Lagarosiphon* are usually fast-growers and will naturally replace any losses quite quickly.

GRAVEL

So far, we have seen that the gravel presents a good camouflaging medium but two other uses for it are: a) as a medium in which the aquarium plants will grow and b) as a filter bed.

Both the colour and the size of the gravel is important. It is best to choose a natural brown-coloured gravel as this blends in with most rockwork fairly satisfactorily, and its dark colour will make the fish feel more secure as they swim over it. Although artificially-coloured gravels are available, the gaudy colours are hardly natural and there is also a danger that the dyes used may be toxic or may leach out into the water.

Particle size should be around $^1/_{10}$ in (3 mm) in diameter, so that plants can root in it easily, water flow through the gravel (in biological filtration systems) will not be impeded and, most important of all, uneaten food will not fall between the particles beyond the reach of the fishes.

ROCKS

Rocks supply a much-needed dramatic effect in the aquarium where the otherwise flat landscape would be very dull. Rocks can help keep the gravel banked up in tiers but large, oversized pieces of rock will restrict the swimming spaces in the tank.

The actual composition of the rocks used must be considered; any rock which is likely to be soft and soluble (some sandstones particularly), or which contains obvious metallic ores should not be used. Rocks with a high calcium content will adversely affect the water's hardness and should also be excluded from the aquarium. Granite, slate and any impervious rocks are quite suitable. It should not be necessary to add that jagged, sharp-edged rocks should not be used, especially in aquaria which are to house fishes with long, flowing fins.

Blending the rocks in with the gravel is an art; it will be almost impossible to obtain matching gravel and rocks but a few small rocks can be smashed to provide a top-covering for the gravel to complete the illusion.

WOOD AND OTHER DECORATIVE MATERIALS

Many fishkeepers like to include wood in the form of logs or tree roots in their aquarium design. Any wood used should be completely dead and free from any rotting. It should be boiled in a few changes of water and also submerged in water for a considerable time to ensure that there is no tendency for discolouring tannins or humic acids to leach out into the water. Wood can also be sealed by a few coats of polyurethane varnish before being used as aquarium decoration.

Cork bark is another popular material. It can be cut to shape easily and forms a most attractive background, but make sure that no fish can get behind it and become trapped unseen.

Wood and cork both share the annoying tendency to float. This can be prevented by anchoring wood logs to a base plate which is then buried in the gravel, or tying cork (with invisible nylon thread) around a gravel-filled bottle or plastic tube to weight it down in position.

Less natural-looking items of decoration, such as divers, mermaids, treasure-chests and sunken galleons, are best left out of the aquarium. They are hardly in keeping with the underwater aquascape you are trying to create and serve no practical purpose either.

10

SETTING UP YOUR AQUARIUM

The setting up of an aquarium needs to be done in a particular order, so that the whole process is neither protracted nor messy. The empty tank is placed in position and then furnished with equipment and materials, building up to the final 'aquascape'. Generally-speaking, the order of preparation is as follows:

1. Site and tank preparation
2. Gravel and rocks
3. Aeration and filtration equipment
4. Water
5. Plants
6. Lighting
7. Electrical connections
8. Switch on and operational checks
9. Adding the fishes.

By now, you will have learned the purpose of the various pieces of equipment, the suitabilities of gravels and rocks, the reasons for providing plants and what type of water to use. This knowledge will enable you to make best use of the materials and there is less chance of you doing things in the wrong order, or using the wrong materials.

1. SITE AND TANK PREPARATION

Choose the site for the tank according to the guidance given earlier (Chapter 3), making sure it is firm and level. Place a slab of expanded polystyrene, cut to the tank's base dimensions, in position on the stand.

The tank should be inspected for leaks, preferably out of doors, before use. Any leaks can easily be cured with aquarium sealant (don't use the similar-looking sealants used in building works, as these may be toxic to the fishes), and be careful to do such work in a well-ventilated area as the sealant gives off a heavy vapour.

If the tank is to be set against a wall, remember to paint the *outside* of the back glass with a plain colour so that the wallpaper won't be visible through the tank. Alternatively, a suitable aquarium backing decoration, or an exterior dry diorama can be used but these must be fixed in position beforehand otherwise the whole tank will have to be moved!

Tanks smaller than the suggested minimum dimensions can be partly furnished with rocks and gravel before being placed in their final positions, but our 36-in or 1-m long tank will weigh too much when decorated with rocks and gravel for this to be practicable.

2. GRAVEL AND ROCKS

Before adding the gravel, a decision has to be made as to whether to use biological filtration or not; if so, the filter plate must be put into the tank before the gravel.

Gravel should be washed thoroughly before use. This is easily done by using a bucket and running water from a hosepipe. Fill the bucket half-full with gravel and agitate the gravel until the overflowing water is clear of dirt. Empty the clean gravel into the tank and repeat the process until enough gravel has been cleaned.

Place the gravel in the tank over the filter-plate to a depth of ¾ – 1 in (2 – 3 cm). Next, cover the gravel with a piece of nylon mesh (to protect the filter from exposure by digging fishes) and place the largest rocks in position. (Where biological filtration is not used, large rocks should be placed directly on the aquarium base before the gravel is added.)

Add the remainder of the gravel and contour it to taste. Slope the gravel, from the back down to the front, with a depth of gravel at least 3 in (about 7 cm) deep at the back. Smaller rocks can be used to form terraces and maintain the slope of the gravel.

Goldfishes are not cave-dwelling fishes and such rocky constructions will be a waste of effort and only deny the fishes valuable swimming space. Try not to form rocky outcrops behind which a fish can become trapped, nor which impede the water flow to and from any filtration equipment.

3. AERATION AND FILTRATION EQUIPMENT

The rocks can effectively hide the aquarium hardware equipment such as air stones and filter pipes. Air lines can be buried in the

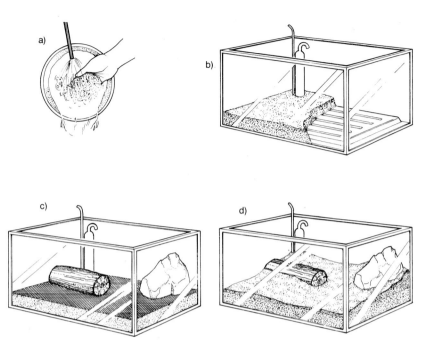

Figure 13. Gravel should be thoroughly washed before use. Wash approximately half a bucketful at a time under a running hose (a) until no more dirt is washed out. Put the filter plate in the tank first and cover it with 2 – 3 cm (about an inch) of gravel (b). Add a nylon mesh (to prevent digging fishes uncovering the filter plate) then place any large rocks or logs in position (c). Add another layer of gravel (2 cm/1 in at front rising to 5 cm/2 in or more at the back); the log and rocks will create terraces of higher parts of gravel for added effect.

gravel. When arranging external filter equipment, try and arrange a flow of water across the whole tank; this can be done by extending the return tube from any outside filters.

The air pump should, ideally, be situated above the water level to prevent any water siphoning into the pump should the pump stop for any reason. Failing this, the pump can be stood alongside the aquarium, or even beneath it on a convenient shelf, providing that anti-siphon precautions are taken (see p. 28).

The control of air to air stones or filters can be controlled most conveniently by a set of air valves stuck to the side of the aquarium. The air tube from the air pump is connected to this assembly and each piece of equipment then fed independently from its own valve.

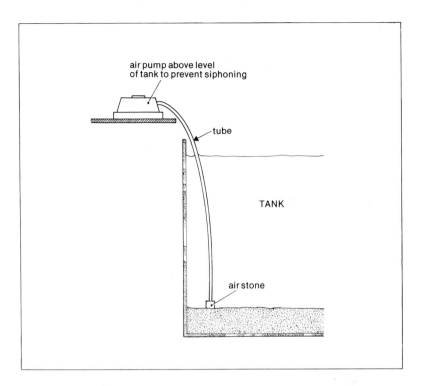

Figure 14. Ideally, the air pump should be situated above the aquarium to prevent water siphoning back into the pump. If the pump is sited below the tank (or below the water level of the tank) then it must be safeguarded by a 'one-way' check-valve which allows air to pass into the tank but not water back into the pump.

Fill the filter box or canister body with filter medium; connect the siphon inlet tubes and return tubes; make sure that any water hose connections to external power filters are securely tight.

4. WATER

When filling the tank you must be careful not to flatten any 'landscape' you have created. Place a saucer on the gravel and let the hosepipe fill this first; the overflow will then gently fill the tank without any disturbance taking place. *Only fill the tank about three-quarters full at this stage:* if you completely fill the tank, when you put your arms in the tank to plant it, there will be an overflow of water, which won't be too popular with the rest of the household!

49

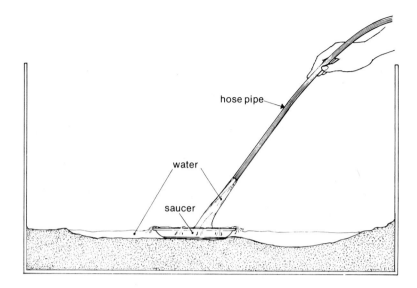

Figure 15. Direct the water from a hosepipe into a saucer or jamjar on the gravel to prevent disturbing the gravel. Do not completely fill the tank at this stage.

5. PLANTS

Before planting, it is a good idea to rinse all the plants thoroughly to remove any snails' eggs and parasites. You can also disinfect the plants by giving them a soak in a weak (pink) solution of potassium permanganate for an hour or so.

Remove all dead and yellowing leaves and trim the roots back a little. Plants purchased as bunches of cuttings should be weighted with thin strips of lead, but be careful not to crush the stems. Do not bury any rotting part of a stem, it will not root. Lay out all the plants on a piece of wet newspaper in species groups.

When planting, have a definite plan to work from and keep evaluating your efforts by a quick glance through the front glass. It is best to work inwards from the back and sides, ending up with the 'specimen' plants. Plant each species in separate groups, not singly (except in the case of specimen feature plants). Plants look better and more natural in clumps.

Plants should be rooted so that the crown of the plant (the junction between stem and root) is just clear of the gravel surface. Protect the crowns of plants with a few small pebbles so that the foraging Goldfishes will not uproot them.

50

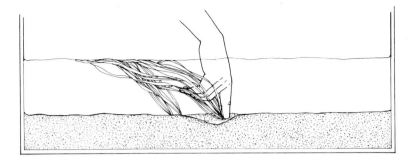

Figure 16. Use a finger to spread out the roots of the plant and bury the plant well into the gravel. Then, withdraw the plant until the crown (the junction between stem and roots) is just above the gravel. Position plants in species clumps, not as isolated specimens.

When planting is complete, the tank can be filled completely. Any dust or scum floating on the water surface can be removed by drawing a sheet of paper across the surface.

Prime the filter inlet siphon tubes and allow the filter boxes to fill with water. After priming the external power filters, reconnect the return tubes securely.

Floating plants should now be added, but there is every likelihood of them spreading very quickly, in which case they will require repeated thinning out if they are not to prevent the light from reaching the plants below.

6. LIGHTING

All light-fittings should be waterproof and the lamps further safeguarded against water damage by the use of a cover-glass. The cover-glass is placed on top of the tank, usually on a small glass ledge running the whole length of the tank, before the reflector/hood is placed in position. It may be necessary to cut the hood and/or the cover-glass to admit filter tubes and air lines.

Make sure that the hood is well ventilated, especially if tungsten lighting is to be used.

7. ELECTRICAL CONNECTIONS

Electrical connections for air pumps, lighting and power filters are best made via a proprietary junction box, e.g. a 'Cable Tidy', fixed to the side of the tank and fed from a single power outlet. There are usually some switched circuits available for independent control of lighting and air pumps, and there will be a warning neon lamp to indicate that mains voltage is being supplied to the junction box. *WARNING: Electricity and water do not mix. Always switch off the supply before placing the hands in the tank, making any adjustments or replacing equipment.*

8. SWITCH-ON AND OPERATIONAL CHECKS

It will be fairly obvious whether or not the equipment is working upon switching on. If nothing works, check that the power is switched on and also check that you have fitted the correct-sized fuse into the plug. The main cause for immediate concern for new fishkeepers is that filters and air stones never seem to want to co-operate. This is easily rectified by carefully balancing the supply of

Figure 17. Float the plastic bag in the aquarium for at least 15 minutes (a) to equalise the water temperatures before releasing the new fish into the aquarium (b).

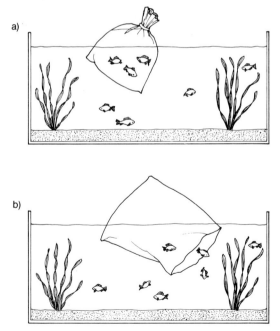

air to each piece of equipment by means of the independent air valves. *Once running, do not switch off the air-supply to biological filters.*

Although it is quite possible to add fishes immediately to the newly-furnished tank, it is better to allow it to settle down naturally for a week or two before introducing the fishes. During this time, the plants will take root (you can test this by gently tugging at them) and the biological filter's bacterial bed will gradually mature.

With the exception of adding food, operate the aquarium just as if there were fishes in it, switching the lights on and off daily. Check for leaks and satisfactory operation of equipment. A nitrite test kit will show the level of nitrite present; this will decrease as the biological filter bed matures.

9. ADDING THE FISHES

Although Goldfishes are coldwater fishes, it is likely that they will still undergo a temperature change on the journey to your aquarium. You can prevent them becoming stressed by equalising the water temperatures before putting them in the aquarium. Either stand their travelling container in the same room as the aquarium for half an hour or so (the aquarium's water will be at room temperature) or float them, in their plastic bag, in the aquarium for a slightly shorter period. When you judge that the two temperatures are equal, gently release the fishes into their new home.

11
FEEDING YOUR GOLDFISHES

The correct diet for a Goldfish is not the same as that, say, required by tropical fishes. It is not just because of the water temperature differences; Goldfishes require a larger proportion of carbohydrates than sheer proteins.

Many fishkeepers with a Goldfish pond will appear to feed very rudimentary foods to their fishes, but you must remember that their fishes' diet is being heavily supplemented by the natural foods found in the pond. Fishes kept in the indoor aquarium have no recourse to natural live foods unless you, the fishkeeper, provide them. Again, the conditions in an indoor aquarium do not follow the conditions dictated by the elements found out of doors; theoretically, the fishes in an aquarium should be ready to feed at all times, as the water temperature does not vary very much from month to month. It could be argued that indoor fishkeepers have therefore to work a little harder in providing a good diet for fishes.

The food for Goldfishes can, like foods for any other aquarium-kept fish, be divided into two types – live and prepared.

LIVE FOODS
The value of live foods cannot be stressed enough. Many fishes, particularly the Fancy Varieties of Goldfishes, depend on the excellent start that live foods give, if they are to become prize-winning specimens. Not all the live foods for fishes are waterborne; there are a number of foods that are of terrestrial origin.

AQUATIC FOODS
The most familiar food will be the Water-Flea *(Daphnia)*. This freshwater crustacean can be captured from ornamental ponds quite easily and it apparently fulfils an important laxative service as far as the fishes are concerned; the actual food value of *Daphnia* is less clear.

Along with the *Daphnia* catch, you may also net another

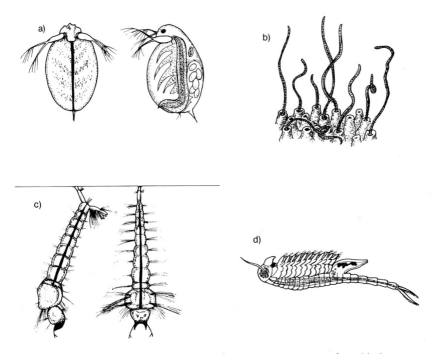

Figure 18. Water Flea *(Daphnia pulex)*, a freshwater crustacean found in large numbers in ornamental ponds during summer and an excellent laxative food. (b) *Tubifex* worms reside in none-too-clean river mud, but if well-cleaned before use make good food for fishes; (c) wriggling Mosquito larvae, found in rain-butts and stagnant pools during the warm months, are excellent food for bringing fishes into breeding condition; (d) freshwater Shrimps, like this *Chirocephalus* sp., are also valuable foods. The eggs from a similar, but much smaller, marine species, *Artemia salina,* may be hatched in warm salt water to provide invaluable first live food for young fish.

crustacean, *Cyclops.* The females can be recognised by the two external egg pouches they carry. Some fish take it readily, others are not quite so keen, and there is a danger that the young of *Cyclops* may attack and eat very young fishes.

If you are lucky enough to find your own source of live foods in a nearby pond, do not catch more food than you need. During warm weather, much of it can die on the way home if it is overcrowded. It is far better to let the live foods continue to multiply in the most natural way and make more collecting trips. Surplus live foods can have the water drained off and then be quickly frozen in the deep-freeze for future use.

As with aquatic plants brought in from the wild, you must screen live foods to prevent undesirable animals being introduced into the aquarium. The larvae of Dragonflies and Diving Beetles can harm young fishes and your Goldfish might also eat small Tadpoles.

The garden water-butt is another good hunting ground for aquatic fish-foods. During the late Spring and early Summer months, there will be a host of Mosquito, Gnat and Midge larvae to be caught. All will make nutritious meals for your fishes which will be a great help in bringing them into fine condition.

Another popular live food is *Tubifex*, a small red worm found in river mud. These are best obtained from your aquatic dealer as their collection is a rather specialised job and best left to the experts. Nowadays, supplies of this food are diminishing because of the clean-up of their natural habitats. *Tubifex* worms must be cleaned before feeding to the fishes; if they are kept in a shallow container under a running tap for a few hours most of the dirt will be washed away. Some fishkeepers refuse to use *Tubifex* for fear of contaminating their fish with disease.

One of the best aquatic live foods is the nauplius (newly-hatched) stage of the Brine Shrimp *(Artemia salina)*. Brine Shrimp eggs can be stored dry for very long periods and can be hatched when re-immersed in salt water. They provide a living, disease-free food of particular importance to newly-hatched young fishes.

Salt water for hatching Brine Shrimp eggs should be made up at a concentration of about 4 – 5 oz of sea-salt to an Imperial gallon of water (25 – 30 g per litre), or less proportionately if you need smaller quantities. Do not use ordinary table-salt as this has additives to make it run freely. Hatching temperature should be around 24 °C (75 °F). Do not worry about their salt-water origin, you rinse the shrimps through with fresh water before feeding them to the fish. Many aquatic dealers sell live *Mysis* shrimp, as well as *Daphnia* and *Tubifex* when available.

Other aquatic-based foods (and this may be thought to be stretching a point) include the raw flesh of any white fish, the meat from shellfish and fish roe.

OTHER LIVE FOODS

Worms are especially good food for fishes and these can be obtained in many sizes from Earthworm proportions down to minute, hardly visible worms.

Earthworms provide excellent nourishment and can be gathered from the garden quite easily. Avoid using worms from areas that have been treated with insecticide or fertilisers. All fishes will eat earthworms, although you may have to shred the worms up for smaller fishes.

Members of the *Enchytraeus* Whiteworm group are much smaller and can be cultured by the fishkeeper. Their sizes range from the tiny Microworm, through the larger Grindalworm to the Whiteworm itself. All are cultured on a cereal-based diet on a compost bed kept in wooden boxes. Grindalworms require a slightly higher ambient temperature than Whiteworms. Initial starting cultures of these foods are obtainable either from your aquatic dealer or from mail-order sources.

Many insects are relished by the fishes and you can experiment with any that you may be able to capture. Do not feed the fishes with insects that have been killed with insecticides.

PREPARED FOODS

The aquatic dealer will stock a large range of dried foods (in flake, pellet or tablet form) suitable for fishes, but you must make sure that you use quality foods that have been specially formulated for Goldfishes' dietary needs. Freeze-dried foods, whose basic ingredients contain many of the live, waterborne foods described above, are another way of giving your fishes the range of foods that they need without any danger of introducing disease into the aquarium.

OTHER SOURCES OF FOOD

You should give your fishes as varied a diet as possible and you can even supplement it with household scraps. Scrapings of raw lean meat, spinach, lettuce, rolled oats and peas can all be offered with some success but fatty leftovers should be avoided.

FOOD FOR YOUNG FISHES

When the young Goldfish finally uses up the nourishment contained in its yolk-sac, it will require food. Naturally, this food must be available not only in sufficient quantities (too much will pollute the tank and cause almost as many problems as too little), but must also be of the correct size.

First foods for fry can be Microworms and Brine Shrimp nauplii. Cultures of these nutritious foods should be arranged on a continuing basis, with new cultures being started so that they overlap with the exhaustion of the old and so provide a continuing supply of food. As the fishes grow, the size and quantity of the food should be increased.

There are many fishkeepers' recipes for providing initial foods, which are all based on encouraging microscopic life in a watery infusion of decaying vegetation. You may have more luck at this than others, the only thing that *can* be guaranteed is a strong smell and complaints from the rest of the family!

CORRECT FEEDING

It is important that fishes are given the correct amount of food. Too little will result in very slow growth (if any), whilst too much food will cause problems too. Fishes will not over-eat, but any surplus food will decay in the aquarium and pollute the water. Only give the fishes as much dried, prepared food as they will willingly eat in a few minutes. It is quite normal to feed the fishes two or three

Figure 19. This perforated floating worm feeder (a) allows surface swimmers to feed from worm foods which would otherwise sink to the bottom too quickly. The worm basket can be removed and the device then becomes a normal feeding ring (b). In either instance, it is held in the desired position by a sucker pad.

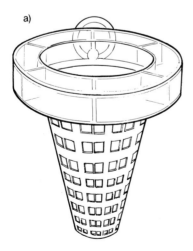

times a day, providing that they eat all you give them each time.

Live aquatic food usually presents no danger except, if too much is given, it will compete with the fishes for the vital oxygen in the water. Do not overfeed with worm foods as they have one or two inherent dangers: Whiteworms are considered too fatty to be fed regularly and *Tubifex* worms will burrow into the aquarium gravel if not eaten. Goldfishes should soon root them out, but it may be better to feed *Tubifex* using a floating worm-feeder to be on the safe side.

If terrestrial live foods are given, these will drown if not eaten fairly quickly and should be removed if the fishes continue to ignore them. Similarly, household scraps should be removed if not eaten fairly quickly; a simple way to feed chunks of food is to thread them on a piece of cotton and dangle them in the water. They can then be easily removed.

12
AQUARIUM MANAGEMENT

It would be wrong to say that the aquarium needs very little time spent on it although, in comparison to other forms of pet-care, the time devoted to maintenance is much less. The rules for continuing success are, primarily, to observe what is going on in the aquarium, perform regular checks and make sure that the necessary chores are not neglected.

CHECKS

The first thing you should notice is whether any of the fishes are missing or off-colour. This check is carried out most conveniently when the fishes congregate 'ready for inspection' at feeding times. A missing fish should be searched for as, should it die unnoticed, its decomposing body could cause problems in the tank.

You can also take advantage of the gathering of fishes to see if any are displaying symptoms of disease or, looking on the brighter side, are coming into breeding condition. If either is the case, then a separate aquarium should be prepared and the fishes in question treated accordingly.

Plant life must also come under scrutiny; if the rates of growth

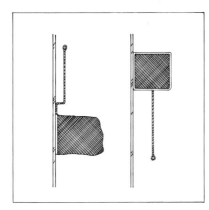

Figure 20. Catching fish is made a lot easier if you use square nets and bend the handle so that fishes can't escape by squeezing through gaps between net and aquarium glass.

60

are not satisfactory, or if there is excessive algal growth, changes must be made to the period or strength of the illumination of the aquarium (see Chapter 7).

Aeration and filtration operations can be checked quite easily, as the column of air bubbles and the water flows can hardly be missed. Any diminishing rates will indicate a clogged filter or a failing air-pump (see below).

Unlike tropical aquaria, there is no requirement to check the temperature of the water. However, in summer months, the temperature may rise quite high and the fishes will appreciate an increase of aeration.

MAINTENANCE TASKS

By far the most important task is the regular partial water change. About 20 per cent of the water should be replaced every 3 weeks or so. In hot weather, the fishes will welcome the addition of slightly cooler water, but generally you should try to ensure that the temperature of the replacement water is reasonably near to that of the aquarium water so that the fishes are not subjected to shock.

When siphoning out the old water (a wide-bore tube is best), detritus can easily be removed at the same time by keeping the inlet end of the siphon tube near to the surface of the gravel, but don't let the tube become clogged with gravel.

Alternatively, water changes can be made automatically by means of water-changing devices that clip on to the aquarium; these siphon off the water and replace it with fresh by means of a double 'supply

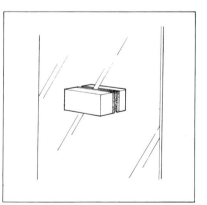

Figure 21. Magnetic algae scrapers can be 'parked' on the glass of the aquarium when not in use; moving the outside one causes the inside part to move in sympathy, scraping off algae as it does so.

and drain' tube connected to the tap and sink. (Water replacement using this method is so slow that any temperature differences between the new water and the aquarium water is negligible.) When using automatic water changers, detritus will not be removed from the bottom of the aquarium and the use of an air-operated 'vacuum-cleaner' sediment-remover is recommended.

Dead leaves should be trimmed back and excessive growth thinned out. Cuttings can be taken to provide more stock. Floating plants must not be allowed to clog up the water surface. Algae growing on the front glass can be removed with a magnetic algae-scraper, a piece of steel wool (don't use the soap-impregnated kind!), a plastic scouring pad or a razor-blade mounted on a planting stick.

Renew the filter medium regularly; there is no point in passing the aquarium water through a boxful of concentrated filth any longer than is necessary.

Remember to clean the air pump's air filter; it is generally located underneath the pump body. If the pump's output appears to be falling, the output air valves (located just behind the output pipe, inside the pump) may also be clogged. Whilst you are checking these, you can also see if the diaphragm is likely to need replacing.

WARNING: ALWAYS disconnect the electricity supply before dismantling any electrically-powered equipment.

Keep the cover-glass and interior of the reflector or hood spotlessly clean; replace lamps as necessary.

13
DISEASES

Despite being in a protected environment, and even under the best of carefully-controlled conditions, your fishes will probably eventually contract some form of disease; fortunately, most are easily recognised and can be successfully treated.

Disease usually strikes at the fish that is slightly below par; stress plays a very significant part in determining a fish's resistance to disease. Stress can be caused in several ways, e.g. bad handling of the fish or subjecting it to sudden changes in its environment. The best way to minimise the risk of your fishes contracting any disease is to follow a set of commonsense rules.

PREVENTION OF DISEASE

Even if you have prepared the most hygienic aquarium for your fishes, with all the correct attention to detail, your fishkeeping ambitions will be doomed to failure if you don't select healthy basic stock. Your efforts at prevention of disease should start at the earliest possible stage.

When choosing fishes, study them closely. They should be free of external wounds, spots, blisters and ulcers. (Scale damage may be self-healing, but it may also indicate that the previous owner has not been over-careful in their handling.) Colours should be dense, with clear definitions between adjoining colours. Goldfishes should fall clearly into one of the three scale groups – metallic, nacreous or matt; mixtures of scale-types are not indicative of a quality fish.

A fish's swimming characteristics should also be noted; it should be able to maintain its position in the water without difficulty and swim without undue effort. Fancy Goldfishes all have distinctive swimming motions that correspond to their particular variety and this should be taken into account. Thin, emaciated fishes are to be avoided and *never* buy from a tank containing dead fishes, no matter how healthy the remaining fishes may look.

The transfer to your home aquarium from the shop represents another stress risk. With coldwater fishes, the risk from chilling is less than for tropical species, but care should be taken to make sure that there is as little difference as possible between the temperature of the water in which the fishes are carried home and that of the water in the aquarium (see p. 53).

Nothing has been said so far about quarantine. With your first purchase of fishes, the initial few weeks in the new aquarium will serve as a quarantine period in itself, but any subsequent additions should be quarantined separately, before they are introduced into the main aquarium. If new fish additions are small (both in number and size), a tank smaller than the main aquarium can be used. It can be furnished with gravel and one or two bunches of plants to make the fishes feel comfortable and aeration, or simple filtration, should be provided. After 2 to 3 weeks, if no symptoms of diseases appear on the new stock, it may be assumed safe to transfer it to the main aquarium.

COMMON DISEASES AND THEIR TREATMENT

Thanks to years of research, the more common diseases no longer present such a serious threat as they did not so many years ago. There are proprietary remedies available from your aquatic dealer that will deal specifically with most recognisable diseases.

With the exception of wounds and some visible fish parasites, the treatment of fishes takes place in water either within their own aquarium, or, better still, in a separate hospital tank. The reason for a separate treatment tank is so that you can administer the correct dose of medication more easily (try calculating the actual water volume in a tank containing gravel and rocks!), and you can observe the fish more closely. Also, some aquarium plants may be damaged by the medication.

The hospital tank can be 'unfurnished', although one or two plastic plants will help give some feeling of security to the fishes. Aeration should be provided (medications often use up some of the oxygen in the water) but activated carbon should be removed from any filter used as it will adsorb the medication. After treatment, before returning the fishes to the main aquarium, it will be necessary to acclimatise them to clean, fresh water conditions once more; the medication can be removed by regular partial water changes until the water conditions approximate to that of their normal aquarium.

Close attention to hygiene will prevent the spread of disease from tank to tank; always have a separate net for each tank. Keep the nets well disinfected, especially when disease strikes – a single drop of contaminated water will undo any successful cures in no time at all. The following brief descriptions of symptoms should enable you to diagnose the disease so that an appropriate medication can be obtained and used.

White Spot

This is an apt description of the symptoms. The affected fish is covered with a number of tiny white spots – these should not be confused with the quite normal breeding tubercles found on male fishes at breeding times. This disease *(Ichthyiophthiriasis)* can only be treated when the causative parasite, a protozoan, is in its free-swimming stage and seeking another unfortunate fish host. Proprietary remedies are safe and very effective.

Velvet

This is another parasitic disease, caused by an organism called *Oodinium*. The 'spots' are much smaller than those described for White Spot, giving the fish a dusty appearance. Proprietary remedies are effective.

GILL AND SKIN FLUKES

Symptoms of Gill Fluke infestation are the fishes' increased respiratory actions with the gills inflamed and held wide open or, in the case of Skin Flukes, the fishes repeatedly scratching themselves against the gravel, rocks or even plants. The Gill and Skin Flukes are called *Dactylogyrus* and *Gyrodactylus* respectively. Baths in methylene blue, acriflavine or formalin are effective. *WARNING: Formalin is a POISON.* You may have to obtain it through a veterinarian and it must be handled carefully.

Anchor Worm and Fish Louse

Both these parasites, *Lernaea* and *Argulus* respectively, are likely to be introduced with live foods or aquarium plants and are large enough to be seen with the naked eye. They can be manually removed with tweezers or killed in a potassium permanganate bath. Treat any wounds caused by manual removal with iodine.

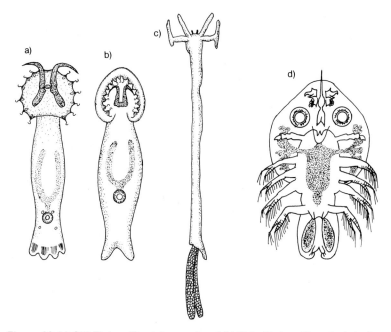

Figure 22. (a) Gill Flukes *(Dactylogyrus)* and (b) Skin Flukes *(Gyrodactylus)* are both irritating parasitic infections; (c) Anchor Worm *(Lernea)* and (d) Fish Louse *(Argulus)* are two external parasites which can be seen with the naked eye. They can be removed with tweezers, taking care not to cause a wound.

Eye Infections

Cloudy eyes, cataracts and eye protrusions can be cured, but there are no hard and fast remedies for specific diseases. Proprietary remedies can help, along with cleaner aquarium conditions.

Dropsy

The symptom of this distressing disease is a swelling-up of the fish's body to such an extent that the scales appear to stand out almost at right-angles from the body. Unfortunately it is one of those diseases that remains a mystery and no known cures for it exist. It may affect single fishes, it can be highly contagious and, sometimes, affected fishes recover unaided. Attempts to draw off the accumulated fluid in the body by means of a hypodermic syringe are not always successful. Affected fishes are best isolated and destroyed if a recovery does not naturally occur.

Figure 23. This overhead view of a Moor suffering from dropsy clearly shows how the scales stand out from the body due to the accumulation of liquid within the fish's body.

Fungus and 'Mouth Fungus'

Body Fungus *(Saprolegnia)* covers the body with tufts of what looks like cotton wool or with a cobweb-like growth. An old-fashioned remedy was to give the fish a short-term bath in salty water, but modern proprietary cures are probably more convenient and just as effective.

'Mouth Fungus' is often confused with Body Fungus but it is caused by a slime bacterium which does not respond to the same remedies. It must be treated with an antibiotic which you can obtain from your veterinarian.

Finrot

The tissues between the fin rays waste away in this disease which is due more to unhealthy aquarium conditions than infection. Proprietary remedies are effective but, more important, a rapid re-appraisal of aquarium management practices is called for.

Gasping

The presence of gasping fishes at the water surface is often taken as a sign of Gill Flukes, but it is more probably an indication of an acute oxygen shortage in the water. This occurs frequently in warm, thundery weather when the oxygen-holding capacity of the water falls anyway, and immediate alleviation should be provided by increased aeration or a reduction in the number of fishes in the aquarium.

'Shimmying'

This is not a disease, but a symptom of chilling. An affected fish will be seen to rapidly and repeatedly weave from side to side when stationary. An increase in the water temperature will effect a recovery. Shimmying often occurs when a fish is transferred from an indoor aquarium to a pond before the water in the pond is warm enough.

Internal Diseases

Whilst the above ailments are fairly representative, there are also internal ailments that affect fishes. The problems with internal disorders are two-fold: a) by the time you notice the fish is affected it is usually too late for a cure; b) positive identification of the disorder is generally only possible by means of a post mortem, when it is most certainly too late to do anything!

Constipation, indigestion, tuberculosis and swim-bladder malfunctions may be all attributed, to some degree, to a poor, unbalanced diet, usually of a fixed type of food. The remedy, if not for affected fishes then certainly for future stocks, is obvious – feed a full varied diet with plenty of live foods.

14
BREEDING GOLDFISHES

Breeding Goldfishes, apart from being quite possible, also allows you to experiment, so that you can improve your strain of fishes by selectively breeding out their defects and breeding in their better qualities. This action is made possible by the fact that Goldfishes will breed readily if both partners are in breeding condition, and many such 'arranged marriages' result in worthwhile offspring. Goldfish-breeders have got this process off to such a fine art that very often the two Goldfishes do not even have to meet! The fish are 'hand-stripped', i.e. the fishes are each manually relieved of their eggs and fertilising milt, which are then mixed together in a bowl before being added to the hatching tank.

There are two main reasons for the development of this form of

Figure 24. Male Goldfish develop small white pimples (tubercles) on the gill cover as they come into breeding condition. Do not be fooled into thinking that your fish has contracted white spot disease when you see these for the first time.

breeding: a) commercial breeders can process breeding fishes as it suits them and b) the more exotically-formed fishes may have difficulty in breeding normally because of the very nature of their exaggerated fin or body developments. Great skill has to be gained before hand-stripping is attempted in order not to injure the fishes by clumsy handling. For this reason, we will concentrate on the more natural way of breeding – letting the fishes do it themselves, with our supervision, of course!

SEXING GOLDFISHES

To take advantage of the breeding potential of the fishes, you must first be able to tell the difference between the two sexes so that you don't waste time trying to breed with two fishes of the same sex!

When the Goldfish is in good health and comes into breeding condition, the male fish can be recognised by the appearance of small white pimples (known as tubercles) on the gill covers and on the pectoral fins. The female will be fatter, due to the build up of eggs in her body, and her vent will appear to protrude slightly.

THE BREEDING AQUARIUM

Goldfishes need space in which to spawn, as the males drive the females hard. An aquarium that holds upwards of 20 Imperial gallons (about 100 litres) should be considered the minimum size for breeding. It is important that the breeding tank should be long and on the shallow side, rather than deep, to allow the fishes ample driving room.

The tank base need not be covered with gravel but there should be dense bunches of weighted-down, fine-leaved plants in which the fertilised eggs can lodge and so escape being eaten by the adult spawning fish. *Myriophyllum, Elodea, Egeria, Lagarosiphon* and *Riccia* are all suitable. Alternatively, bunches of nylon wool can be used (make sure the colour dye is fast by boiling the wool first).

Water temperature is not critical but better results are achieved at around 60°F (16°C). This temperature can be attained by using a thermostat and heater system as found in tropical aquariums. The temperature can be increased further to 71°F (22°C) for the raising of the fry.

glass partition

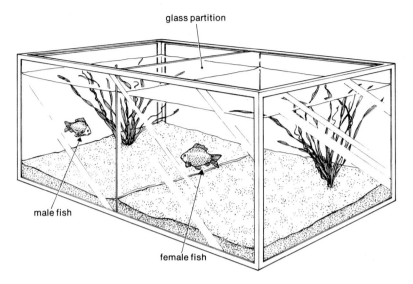

male fish

female fish

Figure 25. One way of ensuring that both fish are ready to breed is to separate them physically (but not visually) for 1 or 2 weeks, during which time they should be well-fed with a predominance of live foods. When they are ready to spawn, the partition should be removed. Ideally, one end of the tank should be filled with dense clumps of plants in which the eggs may become trapped, but these have been omitted for the sake of clarity.

SELECTING AND CONDITIONING THE BREEDING FISHES

It is vital, if you want good-quality, healthy fry, to breed only from the best parent fishes that you have. You should select the two fishes for their combined good qualities; one fish may have the best colours, the other may be the biggest or have better fins. All of these qualities (as well as any defects) will be distributed amongst the fry, which may then be subjected to further quality selection as they grow.

There is no point in expecting the best results from breeding if the fishes are not in the peak of condition when you put them together. To ensure that this is so, the fishes must be conditioned for a period of 2 weeks or so before the actual spawning is attempted.

Conditioning ensures that the fishes are ripe for spawning; the female will fill up with eggs and the male with fertilising milt. Each fish should be conditioned separately (to prevent any unseen spawning occurring), but this can conveniently occur in the

71

spawning aquarium, if the tank is divided into two sections, so that the fish cannot have access to each other. A piece of glass cut to the cross-sectional dimensions of the tank will suffice as a partition. Opinions vary as to whether the fish should be able to see each other during the conditioning period. If you wish to spawn several fishes collectively, males and females may be conditioned as separate groups.

The main factor that will ensure the very best-conditioned fishes is a diet of high-quality, predominantly live foods during the enforced separation. You will soon see the first signs of breeding conditions appearing in the fishes, as shown on p. 69.

SPAWNING AND AFTER

The fishes should be introduced to the spawning tank (or the dividing glass removed) in the evening and the male should soon begin to show signs of interest in the female. Spawning should start in earnest the next day with the male driving and butting the female into the clumps of plants, where eggs are then laid and fertilised; the eggs are sticky and will adhere to the plant leaves. After spawning activity has ceased, the adult fishes should be removed to prevent them eating the eggs.

Many fishkeepers add some methylene blue to the water at this stage. This serves two purposes: a) it acts as a bactericide, preventing fungus attacking the eggs and b) it cuts down the amount of light entering the tank. Shading the tank and being careful about keeping the water clean probably does the job just as well, and obtaining methylene blue is no longer easy.

The eggs hatch after about 3 – 4 days and the young fry then absorb their yolk-sac for another 2 – 3 days before becoming free-swimming. There is no point in adding food to the breeding tank until the fish are ready or need to feed as it will only pollute the water. Once the fishes hatch out, it is time to prepare the live food cultures (most of them take a couple of days) so that food is available when the fishes need it.

First foods for fry can be either a hard-boiled egg yolk squeezed out through a cloth into the water (to give a cloud of minute food particles) or one of the proprietary liquid fry foods. It is important not to overfeed and partial changes of water, along with aeration and filtration (through a simple sponge filter), will all help to keep the water conditions clean. As the fishes grow, the food size can be gradually increased, the best second-stage foods being newly-hatched Brine Shrimp and Microworms. Screened (for size) *Daphnia* and mashed-up Whiteworm can follow.

You will notice that a few of the fry are misshapen or slow developers. You should be hard-hearted at this stage and discard them; be content to raise only a few good fishes rather than many fishes of dubious quality.

Goldfishes generally change colour, from the bronze of their early days to the expected (!) colours of their parents, at around the age of 3 – 5 months. Not all will change at this time; some take longer, others never change at all.

15
VARIETIES OF GOLDFISHES

A non-fishkeeper's idea of a Goldfish is simply that – a gold fish; it will be a standard fish-shape with red or orange shiny scales and nothing much else about it to stir the imagination or get excited about. As for looking after it – well, all you need is a tank, some waterweeds and a packet of 'ants' eggs'.

Studying the above suppositions, they are only about 40 per cent correct; the basic description of the fish may be approximately right, but the rest of the information is surely based on facts that almost belong in the Ark! Having come up to date by reading this book so far, you are now in the right frame of mind to meet the fishes themselves and you will, no doubt, be glad to know that all the previous work will be well worth the trouble; there is a wide range of varieties of the Goldfish for you to choose from.

The different fin developments, colours and 'scale-types' have been classified and fixed by organisations devoted to the culture of the Goldfish and it is very important that these strains are kept as pure as possible; fishes not conforming to these Standards will never be regarded as quality specimens, even if they are bursting with health and vigour; they will never rise above the 'family pet' status in the eyes of serious breeders. Therefore, it would be a waste of your time to breed fishes which do not conform. Fancy Goldfishes are generally divided into two main groups – Singletails and Twintails – the second group being more suited to the experienced fishkeeper.

You would do well to choose wisely and not plunge straight into the more exotic Fancy Varieties, but gain experience with the more hardy, but nonetheless attractive varieties first.

Singletails

Fishes in this group have the 'normal' finnage in that the caudal and anal fins are single fins. The only fin development in these fishes is to be found in the Bristol Shubunkin and the Comet varieties. All the fishes in this group are hardy and can be kept successfully in the indoor aquarium or pond; they are quite able to withstand outdoor frosts in winter.

Common Goldfish and London Shubunkin

The main differences between these two fishes are the colour and the type of reflectivity. The Common Goldfish is predominantly a metallic, red-orange fish although mixed coloured fishes, with yellow, red, silver, white and black in various combinations, also exist.

The London Shubunkin lacks the metallic finish of the Common Goldfish but makes up for this in the variety of colours that show through the scales. Bright blue is a desirable main colour, with red, brown, yellow, black and violet also appearing. There is also some degree of black speckling over the entire body. The colours are not confined to the actual body only, but extend into the fins.

The body profile of both fishes is identical; the curve of the dorsal (top) surface of the body should be matched by the ventral (undersurface) contour. The fish should have a well-built, solid appearance.

The fins are not extra-developed in any way and the round-tipped

Figure 26. London Shubunkin: basically a multi-coloured form of the Common Goldfish, Various colours show through, depending on the degree of pigment in the skin and the opacity of the scales.

caudal fin is not forked too deeply. Unlike the fins of the more exotic varieties described later, the fins are carried quite stiffly.

Bristol Shubunkin

The first thing you notice about the Bristol Shubunkin is the caudal fin which is larger than that of the London Shubunkin and has bigger upper and lower lobes; these should be carried easily without drooping under their own weight.

Colours are similar to the London Shubunkin but the fins are longer and more developed. The dorsal fin is much taller – almost as tall as the body is deep. The body is not so chunky as in the foregoing varieties and has a slimmer and more streamlined appearance.

Figure 27. Bristol Shubunkin: this variety also has multicolours, but here the main feature is the much larger, broad-lobed caudal fin.

Comet

The Comet is a slim fish and can swim very fast for short distances.
Once again, the emphasis is on caudal development. The caudal

76

Figure 28. Comet: a slim fish with a very well-developed, deeply-forked caudal fin. A variety has been aquarium-bred with a 'red cap', the Tancho Comet.

fin is extremely deeply forked and may be as long again as the body.

Pale yellow is a common colour for this metallic fish, although there is a variety (the Tancho Singletail or Redcap Comet) which has a white body with a red cap to the head.

TWINTAILS

Fishes in this group are much more delicate and although they may be kept in an outdoor pond during summer months, they should be brought inside during the winter.

It is with the Twintails that the serious Goldfish-breeder comes into his or her own. To get the perfect specimen in any one of the following varieties means many years of dedicated hard work, patience and good fortune. Very good aquarium (or pond) conditions are necessary to preserve the delicate fins from bacterial attack; each fish must be carefully scrutinised for imperfections, for any that slip through unnoticed are bound to be the major feature of the best spawning you'll ever achieve! Fishkeepers who take this difficult, but hopefully satisfying, road usually restrict their efforts to one or two varieties only – each one could be a full-time job in itself.

The emphasis of development changes from fish to fish throughout this group, depending on variety: it may be body shape, scale development, fin development, colour or eye development – there is something here for everyone.

Jikin

The Jikin is a development from the Wakin (the Japanese double-tailed equivalent to the Common Goldfish). Known as the Butterfly Tail, its caudal fin is best seen from behind – it is 'X' shaped – and, in the best specimens, it stands out almost at right-angles to the caudal peduncle.

It is a metallic silver and red form, and the ideal fish will be silver-

Figure 29. Jikin: a Japanese variety originally, the caudal fin is held very stiffly and at right-angles to the body.

bodied with red fins and lips. You can imagine that this ideal combination is not frequently achieved and is many a fishbreeder's ambition.

Fantail

In complete contrast to the Singletails, the Fantail is a shorter, egg-shaped fish (the caudal peduncle is very short) but, as the name implies, the attraction lies with the caudal fin. This is a double fin (split vertically when viewed from the rear), only shallowly forked but carried fairly rigidly with no suspicion of drooping. The anal fin is also double. The dorsal fin is quite tall.

Fantails can be either metallic or nacreous, and the red variety is very attractive. A further development has created strains of Fantails with normal or telescopic eyes.

Figure 30. Fantail: a short-bodied fish, where the accent has been concentrated on the caudal fin.

Figure 31. Veiltail: another egg-shaped body; the caudal fin has been encouraged to grow in well-arranged, decorative folds.

Veiltail

Another egg-shaped fish, the Veiltail has a down-turned, short caudal peduncle whose line is continued into the flowing, square-ended double caudal fin. The very deep body is nicely balanced by the high dorsal fin, which is set in at the highest part of the dorsal surface. This variety is also found in normal-eyed, telescopic-eyed, nacreous and metallic forms.

Naturally, the fishkeeper specialising in these fishes will want to keep them in the aquarium rather than a pond, so that he can see them as often as their beauty demands, and also where their delicate fins are safe from damage.

80

Figure 32. Pearlscale: each scale on this fish is dome-shaped with a light-coloured centre. The fish has a 'knobbly scale' appearance.

Pearlscale

As its name suggests, the interesting feature of the Pearlscale is its scales. The centre of each scale is domed and light-coloured; this, combined with each scale's darker outer edge, gives the scale a

81

'mother-of-pearl' effect as the light is reflected from them.

The body is very fat (the scale effect is reminiscent, more than a little, of the symptoms of Dropsy) and the fins are similar to those of the Fantail, although the shallow caudal fin is not so large.

It is a hardy fish and, like the Veiltail, is seen to better effect in the aquarium. It is usually found in red metallic forms.

Tosakin

The popular name of Peacock Tail suits this fish very well. Its caudal fin is carried in a very similar fashion to the tail of the Peacock bird, the fin being held vertically across the rear of the fish, then sweeping forward and down on each side.

A metallic fish, the very ornamental Tosakin may have to be hand-stripped as it is not a very able swimmer and can find spawning a difficult act to complete.

Figure 33. Tosakin: in complete contrast to the Jikin's rather elementary caudal fin, here the caudal is a complex set of flowing curves.

Moor

Imagine a telescope-eyed Veiltail in body shape and finnage, but substitute velvety black for the body colour, and you have the Moor. Inaccurately called the Black Moor by many (to Goldfish-keepers, Moors are never anything but black), it is often difficult to see that this fish belongs to the metallic group – except when a little unwanted gold colour appears on the body! This fish is often held in very high regard by coldwater fishkeepers.

Figure 34. Moor: a velvety, jet-black fish whose body shape is identical to the Fantail. The eyes protrude from the head, often attracting the name 'Telescope-eyed' Moor.

Oranda

This variety is also almost identical to the Veiltail except for one detail. Over the head of the Oranda, there is a raspberry-like growth, known to fishkeepers as the 'hood'. In prizewinning specimens the hood covers the head entirely, leaving only the eyes and mouth visible.

A metallic form, there is (similar to the Comet) a Tancho Oranda, where the body of the fish is white and the hood red.

83

Figure 35. Oranda: an added attraction to the flowing fins is the development of a raspberry-like growth over the fish's head.

Lionhead

The Lionhead is a development from the Oranda – if you consider the breeding-out of such a fundamental organ as a dorsal fin a development. Here we have a metallic fish with the raspberry-like growth on its head, no dorsal fin and a short, stiffly-held double caudal fin. There is no 'turn-down' to the caudal peduncle and the dorsal surface has only a smooth, shallow curve. This is the Western world fishkeeper's definition of the Lionhead, for there are many other varieties, particularly in Japan, where each geographical area appears to have developed its own Standard for this fish.

Figure 36. Lionhead: very similar to the Oranda in shape and head growth, this fish lacks a dorsal fin.

Figure 37. Ranchu: the original 'Egg Fish' from Japan. The caudal peduncle is severely turned down in good specimens.

Ranchu

This is a Japanese version of the Lionhead. The caudal peduncle is severely turned down; the more the turn-down angle approaches a right-angle the better, according to the Standard.

Pompon

Apparently a fast-disappearing variety, the Pompon at first glance resembles the Lionhead. However, a closer look reveals that the 'hood' is missing but the fish carries two fluffy 'pompons' on its nose. These are formed from the tissue that divides each of the fish's nostrils; on extremely fine examples they may become repeatedly sucked in and blown out of the fish's mouth as it breathes! Depending on the area of culture, the Pompon may or may not have a dorsal fin.

During its more popular phase the fish was available in metallic and nacreous forms. Obviously, with its peculiar physical characteristics, it is more suited to aquarium life.

Figure 38. Pompon: the fish gets its popular name from the two prominent, over-developed nasal septa, which bounce about as the fish swims.

Figure 39. Celestial: all 'abnormal' features of Fancy Goldfish are brought about by deliberate aquarium breeding programmes. Here, a fish has been developed having permanently upturned eyes.

Celestial

If you spend a lot of time looking at fish in a pond, the Celestial is a variety of Goldfish which may be considered to be getting some of its own back!

Again, similar to the Lionhead in body shape and finnage, but lacking the hood, the difference is with the eyes – they are upward-looking. This means that the fish is at a disadvantage when it comes round to feeding time and catching free-swimming live foods must be very trying for it. A floating worm-feeder will be much appreciated.

This metallic or nacreous fish is best kept in the aquarium with fishes of its own variety in order to give it some peace of mind.

Figure 40. Bubble-eye: a further development to the Celestial. The eyes have extra-large, very delicate fluid-filled sacs beneath them.

Bubble-eye

Like the Celestial (and similar to it in most respects), the Bubble-eye is another metallic fish with an extraordinary development of the eyes. This time, there are large liquid-filled sacs beneath each eye which wobble about as the fish swims. Obviously these sacs are most vulnerable and so the aquarium should be free from any sharp rocks which could inflict damage. This is another fish best kept with others of the same variety in the relative safety of the indoor aquarium.

USEFUL ADDRESSES

United Kingdom

Association of Midland Goldfish Keepers, Miss E.J. Edmunds, 71 Booths Lane North, Boothville, Northampton NN3 2JH.

Federation of British Aquatic Societies, Mrs S. Brown (Gen. Secretary), 46 Airthrie Road, Goodmayes, Ilford, Essex.

Goldfish Society of Great Britain, Mr A.C. Barnes, 10 Lower Forlington Road, Forlington, Portsmouth, Hants.

Northern Goldfish and Pondkeepers' Society, Mrs P. Hodgkinson, 9 Stratford Close, Farnworth, Bolton, Lancs.

United States of America

The Goldfish Society of America, Betty Papanek, P.O. Box 1367, South Gate, California 90280.

REFERENCES

BOOKS

General
Dal Vasco *et al.* (1975) *Life in the Aquarium* Octopus, London.
Favre, H. (1978) *Dictionary of the Freshwater Aquarium* Ward Lock Ltd, London.
Federation of British Aquatic Societies (1977) *National Showfish Goldfish Standards* Federation of British Aquatic Societies, London.
Hunman, P., Milne, A. & Stebbing, P. (1981) *The Living Aquarium* Ward Lock Ltd, London.
Mills, D. (1981) *Illustrated Guide to Aquarium Fishes* Kingfisher Books/Ward Lock Ltd, London.
Mills, D. (1984) *Fishkeeper's Guide to Coldwater Fishes* Salamander Books, London.
Norman, J.R. (1975) *A History of Fishes* 3rd edition. Edited by Greenwood, P.H. Ernest Benn, London.
Sterba, G. (1983) *The Aquarist's Encyclopedia* Blandford Press, Poole, Dorset.
Whitehead, P. (1975) *How Fishes Live* Elsevier Phaidon, Phaidon Press, London.

Aquarium Technology
Jenno, A. (1976) *Aquarium Technology* Barry Shurlock, Winchester.
Spotte, S.H. (1979) *Fish & Invertebrate Culture: Water Management in Closed Systems* Wiley Interscience, Chichester, Sussex.
Sterba, G. (1967) *Aquarium Care* Studio Vista, London.

Diseases
Duijn, C. van (1973) *Diseases of Fishes* 3rd edition, Butterworth, London.

Goldfish

Heritage, B. (1981) *Ponds and Water Gardens* Blandford Press, Poole, Dorset.

Matsui, Y. (1972) *Goldfish Guide* Pet Library, London.

Orme, F.W. (1979) *Fancy Goldfish Culture* Saiga Publishing Co., Hindhead, Surrey.

Teitler, N. (1982) *Book of Goldfish* T.F.H. Publications, New Jersey, USA.

Plants

Jacobsen, N. (1979) *Aquarium Plants* Blandford Press, Poole, Dorset.

Muhlberg, H. (1982) *The Complete Guide to Water Plants* E.P. Publishing, Wakefield.

Rataj, K. & Horeman, T.J. (1977) *Aquarium Plants: Their Identification, Cultivation and Ecology* T.F.H. Publications, New Jersey, USA.

Perry, F. (1981) *The Water Garden* Ward Lock Ltd, London.

Thabrew, W.V. de (1982) *Popular Coldwater Aquarium Plants* Thornhill Press, Cheltenham.

PERIODICALS

The Aquarist and Pondkeeper (Monthly. Buckley Press, London and Brentford, England.)

The Aquarium (Monthly. Pet Books Inc., Maywood, New Jersey, USA.)

Practical Fishkeeping (Monthly. EMAP National Publications, Peterborough, England.)

Tropical Fish Hobbyist (Monthly. TFH Publications, New Jersey, USA.)

Freshwater and Marine Aquarium (Monthly. R/C Publications, Sierra Madre, California.)

INDEX

Numbers in *italics* refer to illustrations.